The Book of Matthew

Save Us Now, Son of David

Andy Nash

Pacific Press® Publishing Association

Nampa, Idaho | Oshawa, Ontario, Canada
www.pacificpress.com

Cover resources from Lars Justinen
Inside design by Kristin Hansen-Mellish

Copyright © 2015 by Pacific Press® Publishing Association
Printed in the United States of America
All rights reserved

The author assumes full responsibility for the accuracy of all facts and quotations as cited in this book.

Unless otherwise noted, all Scripture quotations are from the HOLY BIBLE, NEW INTERNATIONAL VERSION®, NIV®. Copyright © 1973, 1978, 1984, 2011 by Biblica, Inc.® Used by permission. All rights reserved worldwide. This book uses the 1984 version.

Scripture quotations marked ESV are from The Holy Bible, English Standard Version® (ESV®), copyright © 2001 by Crossway, a publishing ministry of Good News Publishers. Used by permission. All rights reserved.

Scripture quotations marked KJV are from the King James Version.

Scripture quotations marked The Message are from *The Message*. Copyright © 1993, 1994, 1995, 1996, 2000, 2001, 2002. Used by permission of NavPress Publishing Group.

Scripture quotations marked NASB are taken from the NEW AMERICAN STANDARD BIBLE®, Copyright © 1960, 1962, 1963, 1968, 1971, 1972, 1973, 1975, 1977, 1995 by The Lockman Foundation. Used by permission. This book uses the 1977 version.

Scripture quotations marked RSV are from the Revised Standard Version of the Bible, copyright © 1946, 1952, and 1971 by the Division of Christian Education of the National Council of the Churches of Christ in the United States of America. Used by permission. All rights reserved.

You can obtain additional copies of this book by calling toll-free 1-800-765-6955 or by visiting http://www.AdventistBookCenter.com.

Library of Congress Cataloging-in-Publication Data
Nash, Andy, 1971-
  The Book of Matthew : save us now, son of David / by Andy Nash.
     pages cm
  ISBN 978-0-8163-5893-9 (pbk.)
 1. Bible. Matthew—Textbooks. 2. Seventh-day Adventists—Doctrines. I. Title.
  BS2575.6.N37 2015
  226.2'07—dc23
                                              2015036166

December 2015

The Book of Matthew

To Dr. Greg King,
fellow traveler in Holy Scripture and Holy Land

Contents

1. Save Us Now, Son of David *(Matthew 1, 2)*   9
2. Called *(Matthew 3, 4)*   17
3. A Twenty-Five-Minute Sermon *(Matthew 5–7, 13)*   27
4. Healed *(Matthew 8, 9)*   35
5. A Kingdom Explosion *(Matthew 10, 11)*   43
6. True Rest *(Matthew 12)*   49
7. Lord of All *(Matthew 14, 15)*   59
8. The Christ and the Rock *(Matthew 16, 17)*   69
9. Questions for Christ *(Matthew 18–20)*   79
10. Jerusalem *(Matthew 21, 22)*   89
11. Christ's Divorce *(Matthew 23–25)*   97
12. Christ's Remarriage *(Matthew 26)*   107
13. Crucifixion, Resurrection, Commission *(Matthew 27, 28)*   117

CHAPTER 1

Matthew 1, 2

Save Us Now, Son of David

A record of . . . Jesus Christ, the son of David.
—*Matthew 1:1*

To understand why Matthew began his gospel the way he did, we might consider the birth of Rick Hoyt.

As he was being born in Winchester, Massachusetts, Rick was strangled by the umbilical cord, leaving him brain damaged and unable to control his limbs. Months later the doctors told the Hoyt family that Rick would be a vegetable the rest of his life and should be put in an institution.

In a profile of the Hoyts for *Sports Illustrated* magazine, Rick Reilly wrote:

> The Hoyts weren't buying it. They noticed the way Rick's eyes followed them around the room. When Rick was 11 they took him to the engineering department at Tufts University and asked if there was anything to help the boy communicate.
>
> "No way," Dick [Rick's dad] says he was told. "There's nothing going on in his brain."
>
> "Tell him a joke," Dick countered. They did. Rick laughed. Turns out a lot was going on in his brain.
>
> Rigged up with a computer that allowed him to control the

cursor by touching a switch with the side of his head, Rick was finally able to communicate. First words? "Go Bruins!" [his favorite sports team]. And after a high school classmate was paralyzed in an accident and the school organized a charity run for him, Rick pecked out, "Dad, I want to do that."

Yeah, right. How was Dick, a self-described "porker" who never ran more than a mile at a time, going to push his son five miles? Still, he tried. . . .

That day changed Rick's life. "Dad," he typed, "when we were running, it felt like I wasn't disabled anymore!"[1]

Dick vowed to give Rick that feeling as often as he could. Four years later, they ran the Boston Marathon together.

Then someone suggested a triathlon.

How's a guy who never learned to swim and hadn't ridden a bike since he was six going to haul his 110-pound kid through a triathlon? Still, Dick tried.

Now they've done 212 triathlons, including four grueling 15-hour Ironmans. It must be a buzzkill to be a 25-year-old stud getting passed by an old guy towing a grown man in a dinghy, don't you think?

"Hey, Dick, why not see how you'd do on your own?"

"No way," he says. Dick does it purely for "the awesome feeling" he gets seeing Rick with a cantaloupe smile as they run, swim and ride together. . . .

"No question about it," Rick types. "My dad is the Father of the Century."[2]

We've got a lot in common with Rick Hoyt, because we too have a Father who will do anything to give us joy. Like Rick, we were all born in a mangled state, strangled by humanity's umbilical cord, paralyzed by the weight of sin. In our own strength, the life we live isn't anywhere close to the life we were meant to live. As hard as we might try, we will never improve ourselves enough. We must be saved from outside ourselves.

Save Us Now, Son of David

It is for this reason that people have always looked up into the night sky for a deliverer. Our spiritual ancestors, the Israelites, had a name for him:

The Son of David.

David—Israel's hope

David, of course, was that ruddy, young shepherd-turned-king from Bethlehem. The people of Israel loved David because he was a warrior-poet. God loved David because he was a man chasing after His own heart. Even David's name was awesome. Pronounced Daweed (meaning "beloved" or even "darling"), its three consonants added up to the special number fourteen—four for "D," six for "W" (V in Hebrew), and four again for "D." The number fourteen was awesome because it was two times seven, God's number.

As a boy in Bethlehem, David was secretly anointed king by a priest named Samuel. The moment this happened, the Spirit of the Lord "rushed" upon him in power (1 Samuel 16:13, ESV). Samuel would later give David this word directly from the Lord: "Your house and your kingdom will endure forever before me; your throne will be established forever" (2 Samuel 7:16).

The throne of David eventually passed to his son, Solomon. When Solomon was anointed at the Mount of Olives, he climbed onto his father David's mule and rode into Jerusalem. The people lined the streets and shouted, "Long live King Solomon." "Save us now, King Solomon." Or put another way: "Hosanna to the Son of David." *Hoshana Lo-Ben Daweed!*

But the celebration wouldn't last forever. Not long after Solomon, the throne of David seemingly came to a halt. With its young princes exiled to Babylon, Israel suddenly had no king, and the people waited anxiously for the return of a King who would once more ride from the Mount of Olives to the shouts of "Hoshana Lo-Ben Daweed!"

They waited 500 years.

Then one day, in the northern part of Israel, an angel suddenly appeared to a young engaged woman. This was the same angel who long ago had appeared to a prince named Daniel, bringing a message of hope: "Seventy 'sevens' are decreed for your people and your holy city to finish transgression, to put an end to sin, to atone for wickedness, to bring in everlasting righteousness, to seal up vision and prophecy and to anoint the Most Holy" (Daniel 9:24).

Gabriel now stood before Mary. The time had come, he told her. The Son of David was about to arrive. Within her.

Jesus—the Son of David

This is why the Gospel of Matthew begins the way it does: "A record of the genealogy of Jesus Christ the son of David, the son of Abraham" (Matthew 1:1). What an impressive pedigree!

Matthew could have stopped right there. That Jesus was the "son of David, the son of Abraham," was all his Jewish readers really needed to know. But for some reason, Matthew doesn't stop there. He apparently thinks there's more of Jesus' genealogy that we need to know about.

"Abraham was the father of Isaac, Isaac the father of Jacob, Jacob the father of Judah and his brothers, Judah the father of Perez and Zerah, *whose mother was Tamar*" (verses 2, 3; emphasis added).

We may have a problem. After such an impressive start to Jesus' genealogy, why would Matthew suddenly write "whose mother was Tamar"? Typically women weren't even listed in genealogies. It wasn't expected or necessary. If a woman were listed, she must have been something special, right?

Tamar was a Canaanite woman who had been married sequentially to two sons of Judah, Er and Onan (see Genesis 38). Both of these sons died in wickedness, leaving Tamar childless. So her father-in-law, Judah, promised that he would give a third son in marriage to Tamar when he got old enough. It never happened.

How did Tamar respond? She disguised herself as a prostitute at the city gate and slept with none other than . . . Judah himself, who had no idea it was Tamar. Months later, when Tamar's pregnancy became evident, Judah took action to have his immoral daughter-in-law put to death—until Tamar revealed to Judah that he was the father of her baby.

What's all this—a soap opera? No, it's the ancestry of Jesus.

Shall we continue?

Save Us Now, Son of David

"Perez the father of Hezron, Hezron the father of Ram, Ram the father of Amminadab, Amminadab the father of Nahshon, Nahshon the father of Salmon, Salmon the father of Boaz, *whose mother was Rahab*" (verses 3–5; emphasis added).

Rahab? It can't be that Rahab, can it? Yes, it can. Rahab was a Canaanite prostitute. She protected the Israelite spies in Jericho and apparently married into the ancestry of Jesus. With fear and trembling, let's move on.

"Boaz the father of Obed, *whose mother was Ruth*" (verse 5; emphasis added).

Ruth was a virtuous woman—but through no fault of her own, she came from the hated Moabites. The Moabites were the product of incestuous relations between a drunken Lot and his daughter after they had fled from the destruction of Sodom.

Are we beginning to see a trend here? These ancestors of Jesus, both male and female, weren't exactly what you would call good stock. Even the mighty David is described as the "father of Solomon, whose mother had been Uriah's wife" (verse 6). As it turns out, even David was a sinner needing a Savior.

Matthew groups the ancestry of Jesus in three clumps of fourteen—the awesome number we discussed earlier. But in actuality, it wasn't quite that neat. There were more than fourteen generations in each of these eras. Matthew seemed to have another purpose in choosing fourteen particular families in each group:

"One gets the impression," writes scholar Frederick Dale Bruner, "that Matthew pored over his O[ld] T[estament] until he could locate the most questionable liaisons possible in order to insert them into his record."[3]

Another scholar, Michael Wilkins, writes,

> The genuineness, and unlikeliness, of this genealogy must have stunned Matthew's readers. Jesus' ancestors were humans with all of the foibles, yet potentials, of everyday people. God worked through them to bring about his salvation. There is no pattern of righteousness in the lineage of Jesus. We find

adulterers, harlots, heroes, and Gentiles. Wicked Rehoboam was the father of wicked Abijah, who was the father of good King Asa. Asa was the father of the good King Jehoshaphat (v 8), who was the father of wicked King Joram. God was working throughout the generations, both good and evil, to bring about his purposes. Matthew shows that God can use anyone—however marginalized or despised—to bring about his purposes. These are the very types of people Jesus came to save.[4]

Why did Matthew go out of his way to highlight the troubled ancestry of Jesus? Because Matthew himself was troubled—a Galilean Jew who paid Rome for the privilege of taxing his own people. What a sell-out.

But Matthew had an important skill: he could write; he could keep records. And when Jesus of Nazareth gave Matthew a chance, he took it. He followed Jesus around for three years, and later he penned the Gospel that would always be first, because it's the Gospel for Israel—for all those who long to shout, *Hoshana Lo-Ben Daweed*! Hosanna to the Son of David!

Jesus came to "save his people from their sins" (Matthew 1:21). That's what an angel explained to a stunned Joseph. What no one fully realized at the time was who "his people" meant. Surely it meant the Jews only. Right?

The Gentiles

There was one more group of people with interest in the birth of Jesus—the Magi. True to form, Matthew seems to go out of his way to include them. "After Jesus was born in Bethlehem in Judea, during the time of King Herod, Magi from the east came to Jerusalem and asked, 'Where is the one who has been born king of the Jews? We saw his star in the east and have come to worship him' " (Matthew 2:1, 2).

It's a great irony that some of first people to seek out the Jewish Messiah would be Gentiles. While most of Jesus' own people (and a paranoid King Herod) thought they knew what kind of messiah to expect, these travelers from the east had open minds and hearts. The Magi, or wise men, were probably pagan priests or respected philosophers from Persia who devoted their lives to seeking for truth—wherever it might take them.

This isn't the first time we find Magi in Scripture. About 500 years earlier, Daniel served in the courts of Babylon with Magi—wise men. Through Daniel's witness, these wise men were exposed to a whole new faith. But the connection between the Hebrew Scriptures and Gentile magic-men apparently went back even further. In the ancient book of Numbers, chapters 22 through 24, we find a bizarre incident involving a pagan prophet named Balaam, who is summoned by a worried King Balak to curse the approaching Israelites. But the Lord intervenes in Balaam's journey, and rather than curse the Israelites, Balaam ends up blessing them. In fact, the Lord gives Balaam one of the most compelling prophecies of a coming Messiah: "A star will come out of Jacob; a scepter will rise out of Israel" (Numbers 24:17).

These words would echo through the centuries. The Roman historian Suetonius wrote: "There had spread over all the Orient an old and established belief, that it was fated at that time for men coming from Judaea to rule the world."[5]

Through the years, many people have cast doubt on whether the Magi really traveled 900 miles to find the King of the Jews. But these types of explorations from the Magi were not unique in this time period. Similar visits of Magi to royalty (though not to infant royalty) are described in Greco-Roman literature. Rather than taking away the specialness of their journey to Bethlehem, this fact adds credibility to the account of the Magi given in Matthew's Gospel.

"There is not the slightest need to think," writes William Barclay, "that the story of the coming of the Magi to the cradle of Christ is only a lovely legend. It is exactly the kind of thing that could easily have happened in that ancient world. When Jesus Christ came, the world was in an eagerness of expectation. . . . It was to a waiting world that Jesus came; and, when he came, the ends of the earth were gathered at his cradle. It was the first sign and symbol of the world conquest of Christ."[6]

The Book of Matthew

What does it say that Matthew's "Gospel for the Jews" includes Gentiles as well? It says that the Lord Jesus is Lord of all. *Hoshana Lo-Ben Daweed.* "Save us now, Son of David!"

---

1. Rick Reilly, "Strongest Dad in the World," *Sports Illustrated,* June 20, 2005, http://www.si.com/vault/2005/06/20/8263519/strongest-dad-in-the-world.
2. Ibid.
3. Frederick Dale Bruner, *Matthew: A Commentary; The Christbook, Matthew 1–12*, rev. ed., vol. 1 (Grand Rapids, MI: Eerdmans, 2004), 9.
4. Michael J. Wilkins, *Zondervan Illustrated Bible Backgrounds Commentary: Matthew*, ed. Clinton E. Arnold, vol. 1 (Grand Rapids, MI: Zondervan, 2002), 9.
5. C. Suetonius Tranquillus, *The Lives of the Twelve Caesars: The Life of Vespasian,* trans. J. C. Rolfe, vol. 2 (Cambridge, MA: Harvard University Press, 1914), sec. 4.5.
6. William Barclay, *The Gospel of Matthew,* The New Daily Study Bible, rev. ed., vol. 1 (Louisville, KY: Westminster John Knox, 2001), 32.

CHAPTER 2
Matthew 3, 4

Called

"Come, follow me."
—*Matthew 4:19*

Sometimes it's the most unlikely people that hear the Lord's voice most clearly.

Six years after I volunteered as a student missionary in the Buddhist country of Thailand, I got the opportunity to do something many missionaries never get to do—go back. Working as a young assistant editor for *Adventist Review* magazine, I returned to Thailand to interview the Buddhist students who had come through our language school that year. I flew into Bangkok and, reuniting with my two teaching colleagues, took the eighteen-hour train ride to the small southern town of Haad Yai, where we'd worked for a year. Several of our students were waiting for us at the train station—the best reunion ever!

Roughly 350 students, most of them teenagers, passed through our classroom doors during that year, and on this trip I found about 35—a tenth. During my week there, I took students aside individually and asked them questions: What drew you to our language school? What did you think of the young foreign teachers who rotated in year after year? What did you think of Bible class? of God? Were the stories real to you or mere fairy tales? What kept you from becoming a Christian? Do you ever still think about it? Do you ever still think about Him?

The students' responses were revealing. Most said they had positive experiences with the little Adventist language school and their teachers. But as sons and daughters of Buddhist families, they were nowhere close to becoming Christians—there was just too much pressure.

I caught up with a girl named Noi who had made our whole year. With bright eyes she had come and studied the Bible, and at the close of the year was baptized in the ocean while we all cheered from the beach. Noi was still there—still a practicing Christian.

As much as this interview delighted me, another one shocked me. A young guy with the cool name of Oood had sporadically attended my Bible class. Though he spoke English well, he never said much. Outside of class he seemed most concerned about having fun—a cross between cool guy and clown. I never took Oood seriously. There was no way *he* was thinking about God.

"You never paid any attention to me," Oood, now an attorney, told me. I sat in stunned silence as he related how God had done so many wonderful things for him, how he had been recently baptized, how he has witnessed to his Buddhist colleagues at work. It was sobering to learn how badly I'd misjudged him.

The timeline

We don't see as God sees. That truth is illustrated powerfully in the story of Christ choosing His followers—twelve ordinary guys from all walks of life: fishermen, tax collector, zealot, faces in the crowd. How could it be that these twelve unremarkable men would someday replace the twelve sons of Israel?

The process of the calling of the disciples is often misunderstood. Many Christians grow up with the understanding that Jesus' call by the sea was the first time He had met these men. That isn't true. Let's consider the full story of how the disciples' calling came about.

In chapter 3, Matthew tells of Jesus' baptism by John the Baptist— how the Spirit of God "descended" on Jesus just as it once rushed on David. Following His baptism, Jesus was led by the Spirit into the wilderness for forty days—conjuring up parallels to the forty years the children of Israel wandered in the wilderness. This was Jesus' preparation period for a ministry that would change the world. Fending off every temptation Satan threw at Him—appetite, power, and presumption—Jesus emerged from the desert powerfully equipped for His mission.

Matthew 4:11 says, "Then the devil left him, and angels came and attended him."

But then, suddenly, there's verse 12, "When Jesus heard that John had been put in prison, he returned to Galilee."

Here's a question: How much time passed between verse 11 and verse 12? A few hours? A few days? A few weeks? From one verse to the next, how much time goes by?

The answer: Probably a full year.

It's true. Between the time of Jesus' desert temptations and His ministry in Galilee in the north, there was an important period of Jesus' ministry that Matthew (of Galilee) doesn't record. In fact, only the Gospel of John records it—in chapters two through five. This was Jesus' early ministry in Jerusalem and Judea.

Here's what happened. After His temptations in the Judean desert, Jesus returned to the Jordan River, where He had been baptized by John the Baptist. Identifying Jesus as "the Lamb of God, who takes away the sin of the world" (John 1:29), John directed two of his disciples, Andrew and John, to follow Jesus instead of himself. Andrew then brought his brother, Simon, to Jesus—a fascinating encounter where Jesus looked straight (*emblepo*) into the soul of Simon and gave him a new name: Peter, the rock. Returning to Galilee with these three men, Jesus also sought out a Greek-named disciple from Bethsaida, Philip, and in turn Philip brought his friend, Nathanael of Cana (also called Bartholomew—"son of Tholomew"), to Jesus. In John 2, Jesus and these five men attended a wedding in nearby Cana—where Jesus performed His first miracle. Then the group of six headed south to Jerusalem.

At this point, the five earliest followers of Jesus—Andrew, John, Peter, Philip, and Nathanael—weren't full-time disciples. They were part-time acquaintances who continued to work their regular jobs.

On Jesus' trip to Jerusalem (see John 2:13–3:21), during which He cleansed the temple courts, Jesus first gave Israel's leaders every chance to become His disciples. In a private late-night conversation with Nicodemus, Israel's teacher, Jesus laid out the mysteries of God's kingdom—and forecast His own death—as clearly as He could. Nicodemus was fascinated but chose to remain in the shadows of faith rather than become what Jesus was clearly offering: the opportunity to become His lead disciple. "If the leaders in Israel had received Christ," writes Ellen White, "He would have honored them as His messengers to carry the gospel to the world. To them first was given the opportunity to become heralds of the kingdom and grace of God. But Israel knew not the time of her visitation."[1]

After the cool reception in Judea, Jesus returned to His home region of Galilee, stopping purposely in Samaria, the Land of the Misfits, for a life-changing conversation. Based on John 2 through 4, we can almost picture Jesus telling His mom back in Nazareth about everything that had happened.

* * * * *

"Well, how did it go in Jerusalem, Jesus?"

"It was mixed, Mom. First, I ran the crooks out of the temple court so the Gentile believers could at least worship there again. That didn't go over too well. But I had a really interesting conversation late at night with Israel's teacher. He's a true seeker, Mom. He has all the tools, but he's nervous about a public commitment. The other leaders in Jerusalem have become very political and secular. Anyway, we left and headed back over to where John was baptizing, but things started to get competitive with his disciples. So we left and traveled north through Samaria."

"What? Samaria?"

"I needed to go there, Mom. Those people matter too. I had a really interesting conversation at Jacob's well with a woman there. She was more receptive to Me than the priests in Jerusalem were! Anyway, I'm going to pull back from Jerusalem for a while. I'm going to develop

Called

these men right here in Galilee. I like them, and I'm headed over to the lake to call them to ministry."

* * * * *

All this happened between Matthew 4:11 and Matthew 4:12.

To Galilee

"Leaving Nazareth," continues verse 13, "he went and lived in Capernaum, which was by the lake in the area of Zebulun and Naphtali—to fulfill what was said through the prophet Isaiah: 'Land of Zebulun and land of Naphtali, the way to the sea, along the Jordan, Galilee of the Gentiles—the people living in darkness have seen a great light; on those living in the land of the shadow of death a light has dawned.' From that time on Jesus began to preach, 'Repent, for the kingdom of heaven is near' " (Matthew 4:13–17).

Zebulun and Naphtali were two of Jacob's sons (see Genesis 35:23–25), and their descendants became two of the tribes that ultimately settled in the beautiful northern region of the land of Canaan. Unfortunately, these two tribes were among the nine tribes of the Kingdom of Israel who gave up their faith in God and turned to idols. These northern tribes were attacked by Assyria, and many of their people were scattered throughout the world—the lost tribes of Israel. In turn, Gentiles were settled in Israel, and Galilee became a mixed population, a confused and dark place.

But as mixed-up as Galilee was, there was this beautiful prophecy in Isaiah—that even in the dark land of Zebulun and Naphtali "on those living in the land of the shadow of death a light has dawned" (Matthew 4:16). Indeed, following the Babylonian captivity, a group of people awaiting the Messiah settled near the harp-shaped Sea of Galilee. The people called themselves the Notzrim—meaning *a shoot* (a messianic term)—and their town became known as Nazareth.[2] This perhaps explains Matthew 2:23: "And [Joseph] went and lived in a town called Nazareth. So was fulfilled what was said through the prophets: 'He will be called a Nazarene.' "

It's interesting—today in Jesus' hometown of Nazareth, most of the population is Arab, and about a third of the Arab population is Christian. This is unusual for Israel. How encouraging that in the homeland of Jesus, many still regard Him as Lord and Savior!

In this forgotten land of Galilee was a small fishing partnership run by four young men: two sets of brothers. These men apparently had a heart for God, because for a while at least two of them, Andrew and John, had followed John the Baptist around. But John the Baptist had pointed them in the direction of another young man from their own region—a man who was sometimes disparagingly called the "son of Mary" because of the rumor that His birth wasn't legitimate.

These fishermen had first approached Jesus of Nazareth—asking to spend time with Him. That's how this culture worked; men would approach a rabbi and ask to follow him. But it was the rabbi who made the final decision about who his disciples would be. And when a rabbi asked you to be his disciple, it was a very exciting moment.

> As Jesus was walking beside the Sea of Galilee he saw two brothers, Simon called Peter and his brother Andrew. They were casting a net into the lake, for they were fishermen. "Come, follow me," Jesus said, "and I will make you fishers of men." At once they left their nets and followed him.
>
> Going on from there, he saw two other brothers, James son of Zebedee and his brother John. They were in a boat with their father Zebedee, preparing their nets. Jesus called them, and immediately they left the boat and their father and followed him (Matthew 4:18–22).

The geography rings true

Each summer for the past few years I've led tour groups to Israel. It's a life-changing experience to walk in the steps of Christ and study Scripture on-site. My favorite place of all is the northern shore of the sweet-watered lake called the Sea of Galilee, only eight miles wide and thirteen miles long. On our morning boat ride, we head east from the northwest corner of the lake toward the ancient town of Capernaum, where Jesus stayed with Peter in his lake house. (Amazingly, Simon

Called

Peter's first-century house has been identified with near certainty; an early church built over it has more than one hundred inscriptions of graffiti containing the name of Christ. Just behind the house are the remains of a first-century synagogue once presided over by the synagogue ruler, Jairus.)

As our boat cruises slowly along the northern coast, I point out some intriguing spots on the lake. Out of the grassy shore a spring of water gushes into the lake. This is Tabgha (meaning "seven springs")—a fisherman's paradise even today. The warm springs produce algae, attracting tilapia and other fish. This site is thought to be the place where Peter and the boys loved to fish—and where Jesus called Peter and Andrew to full discipleship.

"Going on from there, he saw two other brothers, James son of Zebedee and his brother John. They were in a boat with their father Zebedee, preparing their nets. Jesus called them, and immediately they left the boat and their father and followed him" (verses 21, 22). Could it have been in the gushing Tabgha spring itself where James and John were washing and preparing their nets? It certainly fits the description of Matthew 4:22. In fact, Mark's account of this day lends even more insight—describing Jesus and His four full-time disciples as continuing on (eastward) to Capernaum, where Jesus would teach and drive out an evil spirit at the Capernaum synagogue, spend Sabbath afternoon at Peter's house, and then after sunset be visited by a host of sick people. The following morning, Mark describes Jesus getting up very early, leaving Peter's house, and praying in a "lonely place" (Mark 1:35, NASB). Even today at the Sea of Galilee, there's an area between Tabgha and Capernaum that's referred to as a "lonely place." Just below is a little harbor and a natural hillside amphitheater with perfect acoustics. A speaker in a boat could have his voice easily heard by hundreds of people sitting on the hillside.

These types of geographic details provide an even greater sense of awe as we consider the eternal God taking on flesh and living among men and women, boys and girls on the north shore of the Sea of Galilee. It was here that Jesus "went throughout Galilee, teaching in their synagogues, preaching the good news of the kingdom, and healing every disease and sickness among the people" (Matthew 4:23).

Ellen White writes,

> Jesus chose unlearned fishermen because they had not been schooled in the traditions and erroneous customs of their time. They were men of native ability, and they were humble and teachable,—men whom He could educate for His work. In the common walks of life there is many a man patiently treading the round of daily toil, unconscious that he possesses powers which, if called into action, would raise him to an equality with the world's most honored men. The touch of a skillful hand is needed to arouse those dormant faculties. It was such men that Jesus called to be His colaborers; and He gave them the advantage of association with Himself. Never had the world's great men such a teacher. When the disciples came forth from the Savior's training, they were no longer ignorant and uncultured. They had become like Him in mind and character, and men took knowledge of them that they had been with Jesus.[3]

Getting the call

The lives of the Galilee fishermen were forever changed when they were called by Jesus. Jesus didn't only tell these disciples that He *loved* them; he told them He *needed* them. These lowly men were given the highest privilege in the world—the gospel ministry of Jesus Christ.

There's one more geographic feature of interest along the north shore of the Sea of Galilee. On the bumpy road overlooking the lake was a tollbooth where the local fishermen flung their taxes to whatever sell-out Jew paid Rome for the opportunity to tax his own people. Little did this hated publican know that one day he too would get an unexpected call to follow the rabbi from Nazareth.

But that's another chapter.

---

1. Ellen G. White, *The Desire of Ages* (Nampa, ID: Pacific Press® Publishing Association, 2005), 231.

2. Allan J. McNicol, David B. Peabody, and J. Samuel Subramanian, eds., *Resourcing New*

Called

Testament Studies: Literary, Historical, and Theological Essays in Honor of David L. Dungan (New York: T&T Clark International, 2009), 80, 81.

3. White, *The Desire of Ages*, 250.

CHAPTER 3
Matthew 5-7, 13

A Twenty-Five-Minute Sermon

> *Now when he saw the crowds, he went up on a mountainside and sat down. His disciples came to him, and he began to teach them.*
> —*Matthew 5:1, 2*

In the book of Exodus, we see God lead the children of Israel out of Egypt, baptize them in the Red Sea, bring them through the wilderness for forty years, work signs and wonders, and meet with them personally on a mountaintop, where He gives them His law.

In the book of Matthew, we see Jesus come out of Egypt, be baptized in the Jordan River, go out into the wilderness for forty days, work signs and wonders, and meet personally with Israel on a mountaintop, where He amplifies this same law.

The same faith

Many Christians see the Sermon on the Mount (Matthew 5–7) as a new "law of Christ" that replaced the "Law of God"—as though a system of legalism was now replaced with a system of grace. But the faith of Jesus Christ was not a new faith; it was the same faith. This wasn't salvation by grace replacing salvation by works. It was *always* salvation by grace. The children of Israel were saved by grace at the Red Sea *before* they were asked to obey at Sinai.

"It's a popular myth that Jews ever believed they were saved by their obedience," says Richard Elofer, a Jewish convert to Christianity and former president of the Seventh-day Adventist Church in Israel. "The Jewish people," Elofer told me in an interview, "don't believe in salvation by works. For the Jews, salvation has always been by faith. Thus, when [Jews today] enter the Seventh-day Adventist Church, they continue to believe in salvation by faith, but the faith is about Jesus. When they were in Judaism, the faith was just because they were Jews. But it is always by faith."

Craig S. Keener writes,

> Most Jewish people understood the commandments in the context of grace (Sanders 1977); given Jesus' demands for greater grace in practice . . . he undoubtedly intended the kingdom demands in light of grace (cf. Mt 6:12//Lk 11:4; Mk 11:25//Mt 6:14-15; Mk 10:15). In the Gospel narratives Jesus embraces those who humble themselves, acknowledging God's right to rule, even if in practice they fall short of the goal of moral perfection ([Matthew] 5:48). But the kingdom grace Jesus proclaimed was not the workless grace of much of Western Christendom; in the Gospels the kingdom message transforms those who meekly embrace it, just as it crushes the arrogant, the religiously and socially satisfied.[1]

In preaching this sermon, writes Keener, Jesus was establishing His "unique authority as the supreme expositor of the law's message, a new Moses."[2]

"Do not think," Jesus Himself said, "that I have come to abolish the Law or the Prophets. I have not come to abolish them but to fulfill them" (Matthew 5:17).

How to view it

Spoken from a Galilean hillside, Jesus' sermon probably lasted about twenty-five minutes—shorter than most sermons at church. It's universally considered the greatest sermon ever preached.

"Perhaps no other religious discourse in the history of humanity," writes Craig L. Blomberg, "has attracted the attention which has been devoted to the Sermon on the Mount. Philosophers and activists from many non-Christian perspectives who have refused to worship Jesus nevertheless have admired his ethic. In the twentieth century, Mohandas Gandhi was the sermon's most famous non-Christian devotee."[3]

With the loftiest of standards, how should we view this incredible discourse? Blomberg cites eight possible approaches:

1. Two levels of righteousness—a lower one for regular people and a high one for clergy
2. An impossible moral standard that drives us to our knees (Martin Luther's approach)
3. Civil ethics/pacifism (Anabaptist approach)
4. The social gospel—a call to bring the Kingdom of God to earth (a view adopted in secular form by Karl Marx)
5. An inspiring but impossible call to a high ethic (existentialist approach)
6. An interim ethic only for the disciples—who believed mistakenly Jesus would return in their lifetime (Albert Schweitzer's approach)
7. An ethic for the future millennial kingdom (dispensationalist view)
8. An already/not-yet inaugurated eschatology; the sermon's ethic is the goal for all Christians but will "never be fully realized until the consummation of the kingdom at Christ's return."[4]

Which of these approaches to the Sermon on the Mount most resonates with you?

Applying the Sermon

"In the Sermon on the Mount," writes Ellen White, "He sought to undo the work that had been wrought by false education, and to give His hearers a right conception of His kingdom and of His own character.... The truths He taught are no less important to us than to the multitude that followed Him. We no less than they need to learn the foundation principles of the kingdom of God."[5]

From His kingdom, Jesus calls us to a righteousness that "surpasses that of the Pharisees and the teachers of the law" (Matthew 5:20). This call serves two purposes. It drives us to our knees, as Luther said, in recognition that our own righteousness is "as filthy rags" (Isaiah 64:6, KJV). Only the righteousness of our Savior saves us. At the same time, with the assurance of our salvation in Christ, we are called to the abundant life He desires for us. By inviting us to purify our minds, to love our enemies, to not worry about tomorrow, Christ calls us to the highest possible standard—but all in the context of God's saving grace that stretches back not only to Sinai but to Eden.

"The righteousness (right living) that Jesus describes," writes William G. Johnsson, "far outstrips the righteousness that the scribes and Pharisees sought to achieve by their rigorous attention to details of the Law. This righteousness goes beyond words and deeds—it reaches to the thoughts and motives of the heart."[6]

This is the most important difference in the teaching of Christ versus that of the Pharisees. The faith of Christ is an internal experience, not merely an external experience. Overlooking the shore of Galilee, Jesus took advantage of the natural object lesson to drive home the difference. "Therefore," He said, "everyone who hears these words of mine and puts them into practice is like a wise man who built his house on the rock" (Matthew 7:24). In the dry season on the Galilean shore, the difference in the appearance of the rock and the sand was almost imperceptible. Reckless builders had been known to build their houses on sand, thinking it was rock. When the rains came, the sandy foundation was revealed, and the houses collapsed. Jesus compared those who hear His words but don't practice them to builders on a sandy foundation. By contrast, the person who builds his house of faith on the rock of Christ will endure even the roughest of life's storms.

A growing faith

Later, from a fishing boat, Jesus continued teaching about a deeply rooted faith in a series of parables found in Matthew 13. In the first, Jesus told of a sower who scattered seed all over—on a path, in rocky places, among thorns, and on good soil.

> When anyone hears the message about the kingdom and does not understand it, the evil one comes and snatches away what was sown in his heart. This is the seed sown along the path. The one who received the seed that fell on rocky places is the man who hears the word and at once receives it with joy. But since he has no root, he lasts only a short time. When trouble or persecution comes because of the word, he quickly falls away. The one who received the seed that fell among the thorns is the man who hears the word, but the worries of this life and the deceitfulness of wealth choke it, making it unfruitful. But the one who received the seed that fell on good soil is the man who hears the word and understands it. He produces a crop, yielding a hundred, sixty or thirty times what was sown (Matthew 13:19–23).

The parable hits hard. The good news of the kingdom is distributed liberally to all, without prejudice. But only the softhearted receive it. And it's only from a deeply rooted faith that we can, securely and joyfully, reach high for Christ's desires for us.

I recently came across a beautiful expression of the Christian experience in a surprising article, "Coming Clean," by Max Lucado.[7] For many years Lucado has been one of the bestselling Christian authors. Adored by millions, Lucado has inevitably, like many Christian thought leaders, been placed on a high pedestal. But in this piece Lucado tore open his soul, revealing his own need for a Savior.

"I like beer," opened Lucado. "I always have. Ever since my high school buddy and I drank ourselves sick with a case of quarts, I have liked beer. I like the way it washes down a piece of pizza and mutes the spice of enchiladas. It goes great with peanuts at the baseball game and seems an appropriate way to crown eighteen holes of golf. . . . I like it. Too much. Alcoholism haunts my family ancestry. . . . So at the age of 21, I swore off it."

At this point in the piece, I thought, *Yeah, that's about what I*

The Book of Matthew

expected—a high-profile pastor's safe confession of youthful indiscretion. What I didn't expect were the next few paragraphs.

> A few years back something resurrected my cravings. . . . At some point I reached for a can of brew instead of a can of soda, and as quick as you can pop the top, I was a beer fan again. A once-in-a-while . . . then once-a-week . . . then once-a-day beer fan.
>
> I kept my preference to myself. No beer at home, lest my daughters think less of me. No beer in public. Who knows who might see me? None at home, none in public, which left only one option: convenience-store parking lots. For about a week I was that guy in the car, drinking out of the brown paper bag.

Lucado told of buying beer on the way to speak at a men's retreat and realizing that he had become what he hated: a hypocrite. "It wasn't the beer but the cover-up that nauseated me," he wrote.

Throwing the beer can in the trash, Lucado resolved to make things right—confessing his sin to his church elders.

> I didn't embellish or downplay my actions; I just confessed them. And they, in turn, pronounced forgiveness over me. Jim Potts, a dear, silver-haired saint, reached across the table and put his hand on my shoulder and said something like this: "What you did was wrong. But what you are doing tonight is right." . . .
>
> After talking to the elders, I spoke to the church. At our midweek gathering I once again told the story. I apologized for my duplicity and requested the prayers of the congregation. What followed was a refreshing hour of confession in which other people did the same. The church was strengthened, not weakened, by our honesty.

This is the simple experience of the Christian faith—of forgiveness, of cleansing, of seeking His kingdom and His righteousness. "Blessed are the poor in spirit, for theirs is the kingdom of heaven" (Matthew 5:3).

The treasure house

Jesus' final parable from the boat was a stirring single sentence. "Therefore," He said, "every teacher of the law who has been instructed about the kingdom of heaven is like the owner of a house who brings out of his storeroom new treasures as well as old" (Matthew 13:52).

The imagery in this parable is that of a Jewish scribe who has been listening to Jesus teach at the water's edge. The life of a scribe centered on Scripture, and to this point, his treasure house has been filled with the Hebrew Scriptures only, the Old Testament. But in this parable something remarkable has happened. The scribe recognizes that the Scriptures he loves are being fulfilled in the person of Jesus. Deep into the night the scribe goes back and forth in his scrolls, discovering Yeshua to be: Lamb, Priest, King, Son of David, Messiah, Immanuel. The scribe adds a second room to his house—one filled with new treasure: the New Testament.

Within this parable we find our Adventist identity as a truly Judeo-Christian church. We celebrate salvation in Christ alone, and we also celebrate our spiritual heritage in Eden and at Sinai. The treasure house is Scripture—all of Scripture. It's the reason I'm a Seventh-day Adventist.

---

1. Craig S. Keener, *The Gospel of Matthew: A Socio-Rhetorical Commentary* (Grand Rapids, MI: Wm. B. Eerdmans, 2009), 161, 162.

2. Ibid., 162.

3. Craig L. Blomberg, *Matthew,* The New American Commentary, vol. 22 (Nashville, TN: Broadman Press, 1992), 93–95.

4. Ibid.

5. White, *The Desire of Ages,* 299.

6. William G. Johnsson, *Jesus of Nazareth,* vol. 2 (Silverspring, MD: Biblical Research Institute, 2015), 39.

7. Max Lucado, "Coming Clean," *Leadership Journal* 33, no. 3 (September, 2012), http://www.christianitytoday.com/le/2012/summer/comingclean.html.

CHAPTER 4

Matthew 8, 9

Healed

"Take heart, son; your sins are forgiven."
—*Matthew 9:2*

My three daughters once playfully made a list of the places they especially dreaded going with me on errands. Their giggle-laden list went like this:

1. Home Depot/Lowes: where they had to stand in very boring aisles filled with very boring materials
2. The Men's Wearhouse: where they had to stand (or sit) among very boring clothes and shoes
3. The oil change station: where they had to sit in a very boring waiting area with scattered newspapers and a TV channel that perpetually seemed to play *The People's Court*.

Admittedly I get a little bored at the oil change station too, and we've solved the problem by heading down the sidewalk to the nearby Salsarita's Cantina for burritos, chips, and salsa. In fact, one of our favorite memories is running through heavy rain to Salsarita's, laughing our soaked heads off. Years later, our youngest daughter, Summer, still talks about this. (Funny how she remembers running in the rain more than our trip to Disney World.)

The Book of Matthew

I love these girls so much and want nothing more than to watch them grow up—alongside Cindy, the love of my life. That's why, a few years ago when I learned that I might have cancer (I didn't), I found myself making my own list of what I most dreaded in life. My list was very simple:

1. The girls or Cindy dying
2. Me dying.

As I reflected on my two-item list, however, I realized that something was wrong with it. It was shortsighted; it was all about our lives now. Was this really and truly what I ought to dread most—the loss of life on earth? I got to thinking about what Jesus would dread the most, and I realized it wasn't the loss of earthly life but rather the loss of eternal life. I realized that Jesus' list of what He most dreaded would look like this:

1. Anyone losing eternal life
2. Eternal separation from His Father.

The gospels clearly tell us this. As a believer in Christ, I reasoned, shouldn't my list at least look more like this?

1. The girls or Cindy losing eternal life
2. Me losing eternal life
3. Anyone else losing eternal life
4. The girls or Cindy dying
5. Me dying
6. Anyone else dying.

Even with its lingering selfishness, this list still isn't easy for me to digest—especially the order of items 3 and 4. My flesh screams out against it. Though I may believe and teach that one person's earthly death can result in another's eternal life, I'm repelled by the thought of that person being my wife, my daughter, or me.

Healed

Perhaps you can relate.

That's why it's important for us to keep our eyes not on ourselves but on Christ. In Matthew 8 and 9, we find a Savior who cares deeply about physical illness and death—but even more about spiritual illness and death.

A leper seeks physical healing (Matthew 8:1-4)

As Jesus walked back down the mountain where He'd described the kingdom of God, He re-encountered the kingdom of Satan—a cold, dark place filled with decaying bodies groaning for redemption.

There a leper knelt before Jesus and said, "If you are willing, you can make me clean" (Matthew 8:2). The Greek word for "can" is *dunamai*—like dynamite. It means full of power. "If You are willing," the man was saying, "You are full of power and can change my life."

"I am willing," Jesus responded. "Be clean!" (verse 3).

In Mark's telling of this same story (see Mark 1:41), some manuscripts say that Jesus was "filled with compassion" at the sight of the leper. However, some early manuscripts say Jesus was "filled with anger." Why would that be? If Jesus was indeed "filled with anger" at the sight of the leper, what would He be angry at? The leper? Probably not, although Jesus' stern warning to the leper may indicate some level of frustration with him.

If Jesus felt anger at anything, it was probably at how sin had ravaged the world He had created. Think of how grief-stricken Jesus would have been to see how far humanity had fallen. We were designed to live forever and ever. Even after sin entered the world, humans lived nearly a thousand years—that's how marvelously we were made. But now, some four thousand years later, humanity was coughing and sputtering. "The average man," writes William G. Johnsson, "was about five feet three inches tall and weighed about 132 pounds. . . . Life expectancy was desperately low, with half the population dying before they reached age thirty."[1]

The bones found in first-century tombs "witness to the diseases that wracked humanity and brought people down to an early grave—parasites, such as tapeworms."[2]

With eyes full of power, compassion, and anger, Jesus swiftly healed the leper. He warned him not to spread this news because it would result in a mob, making ministry more difficult for Jesus. The healed man spread the news anyway.

A Gentile seeks physical healing for his servant (Matthew 8:1-13)

A centurion was a Roman military officer who typically came up from within the ranks and oversaw eighty to a hundred soldiers. Because a Roman soldier would serve in the military for two decades, he was not permitted to have a legal family. With, perhaps, his servant as his only real family, the centurion's concern seemed to be deeper than a prospective economic loss, especially given that centurions made fifteen times more money than a common soldier did.

To Jews, the only person more despised than a Gentile would have been a leper, so this Gentile officer, perhaps, assumed that this Jewish Jesus wouldn't want to enter his home—even though Jesus said He would. By asking just for Jesus' word, not His actual presence, in healing his servant, the centurion demonstrated great faith that speaks to us today: Jesus' word is as powerful as His touch. To this centurion, for Jesus to heal someone wasn't a difficult thing at all. It was akin to a military officer giving orders to a soldier—which happened all the time.

Jesus commended the Gentile centurion for having a faith so great that he didn't need to plead. He simply *asked*, and he trusted Jesus to do what was best. Jesus was "astonished" by the centurion's faith—and the servant was "healed at that very hour" (Matthew 8:13).

Excavations at Capernaum where this encounter took place have revealed a military garrison. So this officer would have likely seen and heard Jesus prior to asking him to heal his servant. Perhaps he even heard (or heard about) Jesus' sermon on the mount. The centurion's compassion for others—and his calm faith—are a model for us all.

Demoniacs seek every kind of healing (Matthew 8:25-34).

In Jewish thought it was the prerogative of God alone to rule over nature and demons. After calming a violent storm with a simple word,

Healed

Jesus stepped onto the eastern shore of the Sea of Galilee in Gentile territory—and Satan's territory.

"What do you want with us, Son of God" shouted two demon-possessed men from a graveyard. "Have you come here to torture us before the appointed time?" (Matthew 8:29).

Mark 5:1–20 and Luke 8:26–29 add details to this healing of the demon-possessed men. The demons identified themselves as "legion." A legion in the military was six thousand soldiers. Wilting before the same Son of God they once worshiped in heaven, the demons begged to be sent into two thousand pigs feeding nearby.

Many have wondered why the demons asked to be sent into the pigs. Some suggest that the demons most detested empty wandering; they preferred a home of some type, even if it was an unclean pig. Another tradition taught that demons were afraid of the water; and Jesus Himself even makes references to demons looking for waterless places (see Matthew 12:43). There were also Jewish traditions which taught demons could be destroyed prior to the final apocalyptical day of the Lord.

But the most natural answer is that the demons knew the loss of the pigs would upset the residents—causing them to drive Jesus away. This indeed happened . . . but so did something else. The healed men evangelized their Decapolis homeland—and Jesus would someday be welcomed back!

"In causing the destruction of the swine," writes Ellen White, "it was Satan's purpose to turn the people away from the Savior, and prevent the preaching of the gospel in that region. But this very occurrence roused the whole country as nothing else could have done, and directed attention to Christ. Though the Savior Himself departed, the men whom He had healed remained as witnesses to His power."[3]

A paralytic seeks spiritual healing (Matthew 9:1-8)

Earlier Jesus had said to the centurion that He hadn't found anyone in Israel with such great faith. But during these same hours there was an Israelite whose desire for healing of the heart was even greater than for healing of his body. "It was not physical restoration he desired so much as relief from the burden of sin. If he could see Jesus, and receive the assurance of forgiveness and peace with Heaven, he would be content to live or die, according to God's will."[4]

The late Adventist pastor Morris Venden often preached about having enough faith to *not* be healed. This is the greatest faith of all—when we look beyond our physical circumstances to our eternal circumstances. Often prayer requests are focused on our physical needs, and God does care about these things. He knows that we need them. But in the Sermon on the mount, Jesus said we are to "seek first his kingdom and his righteousness" (Matthew 6:33). We can probably all think of someone who may have a physical disability, yet who maintains a strong faith in God.

We don't always know God's will for *physical* healing, but we do always know His will for *spiritual* healing. "When we pray for earthly blessings, the answer to our prayer may be delayed, or God may give us something other than what we ask for, but not so when we ask for deliverance from sin. It is His will to cleanse us from sin, to make us His children, and to enable us to live a holy life."[5]

After healing this man spiritually with the cleansing words of forgiveness, Jesus added a bonus: complete physical healing. "And the man got up and went home" (Matthew 9:7).

Disciples seek a new life (Matthew 8:18-22)

Embedded within many more healings in Matthew 8 and 9—including that of a bleeding woman and a dead daughter—is the call to be part of the healing ministry of Christ. In Matthew 8:18–22, two men approached Jesus with the desire to be His disciples. Both men were sincere, yet held back by something. Jesus, who knows all, went straight to the heart of the matter. He questioned whether the first man was really willing to give up everything—including his own bed—to follow Him. Jesus then asked the second man whether he was truly willing to put Jesus ahead of his own family.

We don't know what happened to these would-be followers of Christ. Did they get in the boat with Jesus, or did they shrink from full commitment to Him?

Healed

We do know with certainty what happened to another potential disciple Jesus encountered by the lake. "As Jesus went on from there, he saw a man named Matthew sitting at the tax collector's booth. 'Follow me,' he told him, and Matthew got up and followed him" (Matthew 9:9).

Is it surprising that Matthew immediately threw a party at his house—attended by Jesus and "many tax collectors and 'sinners' " (verse 10)? Not at all. We can only wonder whether the partygoers also included those who were healed in these chapters: the leper, the paralytic, the centurion, the daughter of the synagogue ruler, the bleeding woman, the blind, and the mute. What a celebration that must have been—like heaven itself!

Questioned why He was eating and drinking with people like these, Jesus responded appropriately, "It is not the healthy who need a doctor, but the sick" (verse 12).

The sick had never seen a doctor like this.

---

1. Johnsson, *Jesus of Nazareth,* vol. 1, 4.
2. Ibid.
3. White, *The Desire of Ages,* 340.
4. Ibid., 267.
5. Ibid., 266.

CHAPTER 5

Matthew 10, 11

A Kingdom Explosion

> *"The kingdom of heaven has been forcefully advancing, and forceful men lay hold of it."*
> —*Matthew 11:12*

True Story 1: An overworked, overstressed father decides to say no to the culture of "got to give your kids everything under the sun." Instead, he decides to give them himself. He takes a humble and enjoyable job in a mobile phone store, which allows him to be home every day by 4:30 and spend the evening with his kids—not with expensive entertainment, but in the simple outdoors.

True Story 2: A group of young people at an evening worship service hear about inner-city youth who don't have decent shoes for the winter. As they exit, most of the young people leave their high-end tennis shoes under the seats of the church, driving home in their socks.

True Story 3: After years of practicing, middle-aged gay men and women say, "You know what? Our identity is not our sexual orientation. Our identity is redeemed in Christ, and by His grace, we are going to carry this cross for a short time on earth and live according to His Holy Word."

True Story 4: Imprisoned Christians in China don't pray to be set free. They pray for the light of the gospel of Jesus Christ to continue spreading in their dark country.

What do all these stories have in common? They're stories of a kingdom forcefully advancing.

A shocking assertion

One of the most powerful and perplexing statements in Scripture is spoken by Jesus in Matthew 11:11, 12. "I tell you the truth: Among those born of women there has not risen anyone greater than John the Baptist; yet he who is least in the kingdom of heaven is greater than he. From the days of John the Baptist until now, the kingdom of heaven has been forcefully advancing, and forceful men lay hold of it."

What is Jesus saying here? Theologian D. A. Carson provides an expanded interpretation: The kingdom of heaven is forcefully advancing with "holy power and magnificent energy that has been pushing back the frontiers of darkness," and while this is happening, "violent or rapacious men have been trying to plunder it."[1]

While there are other possible interpretations of these verses, clearly three things are happening here:

1. There is some type of violent controversy involving the kingdom of heaven. You might even call it a "great controversy."
2. The center of this controversy is a bronzed, muscular thirty-year-old son of a carpenter from Hickville who has the audacity to refer to Himself as the Son of Man—a Messianic reference.
3. This Son of Man is declaring that everything on earth has now changed with His arrival—that He apparently has set up His own kingdom and that anyone who joins in His kingdom from that point forward will be greater than anyone who went before them, including His cousin, John the Baptist.

Wow!

Jesus spoke these powerful words during a period of intense action. Following the healings He performed in Matthew 8 and 9, Jesus "called

A Kingdom Explosion

his twelve disciples to him and gave them authority to drive out evil spirits and to heal every disease and sickness" (Matthew 10:1). Jesus sent the disciples out in pairs (Mark 6:7)—a wise model in ministry today as well. The pairs were: the brothers Simon and Andrew, the brothers James and John, Philip and Bartholomew, Thomas and Matthew "the tax collector" (Matthew 10:3), James son of Alphaeus and Thaddaeus, Simon the Zealot and Judas Iscariot.

It's interesting that Matthew includes only his own occupation—a tax collector. It was probably best, at this point, that he wasn't paired with Simon the Zealot—who hated Rome and anyone associated with it. Simon was, instead, paired with Judas.

While His disciples were out learning the ropes, Jesus was confronted by the disciples of John the Baptist. John's disciples were perplexed that their leader was rotting in prison—and they began to question the messiahship of Jesus Himself: "Are you the one who was to come," they asked, "or should we expect someone else?" (Matthew 11:3).

Unruffled by the expression of doubt, Jesus sent a loaded message back to John: "The blind receive sight, the lame walk, those who have leprosy are cured, the deaf hear, the dead are raised, and the good news is preached to the poor. Blessed is the man who does not fall away on account of me" (verses 5, 6). Back in prison, John unpacked the message. Jesus was using the language of Jubilee, the fiftieth year of the Jewish calendar when everything was reset and restored. Jesus was declaring that He is our Jubilee. Wherever He was, things were set right. He was the Messiah—and no, John and his disciples shouldn't expect anyone else.

Following His words of reassurance to John, Jesus began to speak about the imprisoned desert preacher. Jesus said that to that point in earth's history, no one had ever been greater than John the Baptist—not a single person. This was an amazing declaration! No one in history—no one born of woman—had been greater than John the Baptist? Not Enoch? Not Noah? Not Abraham? Not Moses? Not David? Not Elijah? How could this be? How could John the Baptist—who ministered for only a short time, who never wrote a word of Scripture, who was followed by just a small group—how could this man be the greatest man to have ever lived? Was he great because of his humility? Certainly that was part of it. But the true greatness of John was the great privilege he had to lower the Lord Himself into the waters of the Jordan River, inaugurating His ministry. No one in history had ever had such a privilege. Our only measure of greatness is our association with Christ. And to this point, no one in history had ever associated more intimately with Christ.

And yet, said Jesus, "He who is least in the kingdom of heaven is greater than [John]" (verse 11). In other words, though John had risen higher than any person before him, the least person in the newly inaugurated kingdom of Christ was immediately greater than John. This is the very reason John's own disciples left John himself to follow Jesus—because the moment they did, they were greater than John. John would never again associate directly with Jesus. He knew his place in the kingdom; he knew he must "decrease" so that Jesus could "increase" (John 3:30, ESV). All who came after John would experience something that neither John nor anyone before him had experienced—direct fellowship with Jesus Christ revealed in fullness. There is no greater privilege.

Two ministry models: Light and salt

Following His declaration about the historical transition taking place from John to Himself, Jesus enters into a more relaxed dialog with His listeners about the way people were responding so apathetically to both John and Himself.

"To what can I compare this generation? They are like children sitting in the marketplaces and calling out to others: 'We played the flute for you, and you did not dance; we sang a dirge and you did not mourn' " (Matthew 11:16, 17). First-century children played games in the public square—their playground. Sometimes the children would play "wedding." They'd act out the parts of the bride and groom and the wedding party, laughing their heads off. Weddings were big three-day celebrations, and you can just picture the children running with it.

After playing "wedding" awhile, one of the kids would shout, "Hey

A Kingdom Explosion

let's play 'funeral!' " Funerals were elaborate events as well, with paid mourners. So the children would sing the saddest possible songs, and other kids would march along wailing.

But in this parable, something is terribly wrong with the children in the marketplace. They won't play anything! Instead, we have the exasperating image of children calling out to other children, "Let's play 'wedding!' " And the other children respond, "No, we don't feel like playing 'wedding.' We're not dancing."

So then the children call out, "Let's play 'funeral!' " The other children reply, "No, we're not playing 'funeral' either."

It's a parable of a completely unresponsive generation.

Jesus explains the parable in verses 18 and 19: "For John came neither eating nor drinking, and they say, 'He has a demon.' [In other words, "We refuse to play 'funeral' with you, John the Baptist."] The Son of Man came eating and drinking, and they say, 'Here is a glutton and a drunkard, a friend of tax collectors and "sinners." ' ["We refuse to play 'wedding' with you, Jesus."] But wisdom is proved right by her actions." Luke's version of this parable helpfully reads, "Wisdom is proved right by all her children" (Luke 7:35).

Jesus' parable provides important insights into two types of ministry, both of them important. The ministry of John the Baptist was a more somber, dirge-style ministry of repentance, of tears, of cleansing. John dressed like the old prophet Elijah had dressed—in camel hair and a leather belt. How could people not see it? John was "the Elijah who was to come" (Matthew 11:14). John's ministry was a call to die to yourself and the things of this world. Even John's baptisms were a symbol of death—of going down into a watery grave. But the people didn't accept John's ministry of death, so they explained it away by saying he must have a demon.

Jesus' ministry was a ministry of life. He came eating and drinking and socializing with people—He came as our friend. He said, "The time for mourning is over; it's time for dancing." But the people wouldn't accept Jesus either. So they slandered Him, saying, "Here is a glutton and a drunkard, a friend of tax collectors and 'sinners' " (verse 19).

Sometimes you just can't win. Like lackadaisical children in the marketplace, Jesus' contemporaries were apathetic and obstinate. They wouldn't respond to *anything*. Their hearts had become too hard. They just sat there!

Jesus longs for us to be as expressive and responsive as children (usually) are. "Don't hold it all in," He says. "Don't lock yourself away. Let Me soften your heart. Let Me cry with you. Then let Me dance with you."

As we think about the ministries of Jesus and John the Baptist, we see two approaches: Jesus' "salt of the earth" approach and John's "light on a hill" (or light in the desert) approach. For example, an inner-city, feed-the-homeless ministry uses the "salt of the earth" approach, ministering to people where they are. By contrast, a rural rehab center for drug addicts uses the "light on a hill" approach, bringing people out of darkness into a land of promise.

"You are the salt of the earth. . . . You are the light of the world" (Matthew 5:13, 14). Both of these approaches are endorsed by Christ Himself in the advancement of His kingdom.

---

1. D. A. Carson et al., *Matthew: Chapters 1 Through 12*, The Expositor's Bible Commentary (Grand Rapids, MI: Zondervan, 1995), 266, 267.

CHAPTER 6

Matthew 12

True Rest

"It is lawful to do good on the Sabbath."
—Matthew 12:12

Let's say that you meet a friend, Dave, at a high school reunion. A few years earlier Dave had married a girl named Stephanie, and you ask him to tell you about her. Here's how he responds:

* * * * *

"Oh, I love being married to Stephanie," Dave says. "And I especially enjoy celebrating Stephanie's birthday. This has been a true blessing from the start. All year I look forward to the celebration of Stephanie's birthday.

"Stephanie's birthday," Dave continues, "is a time when I can just stop everything else I'm doing and focus on Stephanie's birthday. On Stephanie's birthday I get to go out to supper, I get to eat birthday cake and ice cream, I get to see a lot of friends, and best of all I'm able to get off work because it's Stephanie's birthday. Stephanie's birthday means so much to me that on her birthday I always pray a special prayer: 'Thank you, God, for Stephanie's birthday.'"

* * * * *

So . . . how would you feel about Dave's answer? What's missing in his moving testimony about Stephanie's birthday?

Stephanie!

Another birthday

More Seventh-day Adventists now celebrate the Sabbath than any other group of people on earth, including Jews. We have the true privilege of being its torch bearers. Celebrating the Sabbath is, in a sense, like celebrating the birthday of the world that God Himself created.

But as special as the Sabbath is to Seventh-day Adventists, it's important that the Sabbath doesn't become another "Stephanie's birthday." Like the Pharisees (who also were Seventh-day Adventists—think about it), we can become too focused on the Sabbath and not focused enough on the Lord of the Sabbath. After all, consider which of the following prayers you hear most often in our churches: (1) Thank You, God, for the Sabbath, or (2) Thank You, God, for Jesus.

It's no accident that just before two important stories about Jesus and the Sabbath (in Matthew 12), we find these words: "Come to me, all you who are weary and burdened, and I will give you rest. Take my yoke upon you and learn from me, for I am gentle and humble in heart, and you will find rest for your souls. For my yoke is easy and my burden is light" (Matthew 11:28–30).

Jesus' invitation could not be more beautiful: "Come to me." Jesus is the Bridegroom gazing at His bride, the loving Father helping children onto His lap, the Friend who's there when you most need Him. Jesus loves you. He *loves* you. He's crazy about you. He wants the very best for you.

What does Jesus mean when He says He will give us rest? Does He mean laziness? Does He mean anything goes? Of course not. Jesus has a very high standard for us; we saw this in His Sermon on the Mount. But a relationship with Jesus is not intended to wear us out. His yoke is easy and His burden light. It was always this way. We are the ones who turn a light yoke into a heavy one—a blessing into a burden.

In Jesus' day, the Sabbath had become a burden. While past generations of Jews had neglected the Sabbath (leading, in part, to their deportation to Babylon), a new generation was determined never to let

True Rest

this happen again. In fact, the Pharisees believed that if all Israel kept holy two Sabbaths in a row, the Messiah would come. Unfortunately, the Pharisees lost sight of the forest for the trees.

> As the Jews departed from God, and failed to make the righteousness of Christ their own by faith, the Sabbath lost its significance to them. Satan was seeking to exalt himself and to draw men away from Christ, and he worked to pervert the Sabbath, because it is the sign of the power of Christ. The Jewish leaders accomplished the will of Satan by surrounding God's rest day with burdensome requirements. In the days of Christ the Sabbath had become so perverted that its observance reflected the character of selfish and arbitrary men rather than the character of the loving heavenly Father.[1]

The Pharisees' obsession with proper Sabbath keeping led to endless debates such as these:

Situation 1: If a hen laid an egg on the Sabbath, was it OK to eat it? The majority Pharisee opinion was that if the hen was a laying hen, then it was not OK to eat an egg laid on Sabbath because the hen was working. However, if a hen was not a laying hen—if it was just a hen being fattened up to be eaten—then it was OK to eat the egg, because this wasn't the hen's primary labor. (There was also a suggestion that you could eat an egg laid on Sabbath by a laying hen, as long as you later killed the hen for breaking the Sabbath!)

Situation 2: Was it OK to look at yourself in a mirror on Sabbath? The answer? No, because if you saw a gray hair you might be tempted to pluck it, and this would be reaping.

Situation 3: If your house caught fire on Sabbath, was it OK to salvage your clothes? You should carry out only one set of clothing. However, if you put on one set of clothing, then you might carry out another set. (By the way, if your home caught fire, it was not OK to ask a Gentile to put out the fire, but if the Gentile was putting out the fire anyway, that was OK.)

Situation 4: Was it OK to spit on Sabbath (presumably asked by a teenage Jewish boy)? You might spit on a rock on Sabbath, but you might not spit on the ground, because that would be making mud—or mortar.

This was the climate that Jesus had entered—unbelievable rigidities that completely ruined the original purpose of the Sabbath as a day to rest from work, a day to worship God and fellowship with other believers, a day where kids knew their parents would be more available to them.

The Sabbath had become anything but restful.

Accusing the Lord of the Sabbath

"At that time Jesus went through the grainfields on the Sabbath. His disciples were hungry and began to pick some heads of grain and eat them. When the Pharisees saw this, they said to him, 'Look! Your disciples are doing what is unlawful on the Sabbath' " (Matthew 12:1, 2).

The accusation of the Pharisees was that by rubbing grain in their hands, the disciples were, technically, threshing—a type of labor prohibited on the Sabbath.

While most of us would probably roll our eyes, Jesus responded in a more thoughtful manner—using reference points the Pharisees would understand. Jesus first recounted the familiar story of the fugitive David taking bread from the tabernacle that was supposed to be eaten by priests only. In that situation, the hunger of David and his companions was more important than a temple ritual intended for another purpose. In the same way, reasoned Jesus, the hunger of His companions was more important than Sabbath guidelines (about threshing) intended for another purpose.

Jesus also cited the work of the priests in the temple on the Sabbath day. The Sabbath allowed for the work of ministry. In the same way, the Sabbath allowed for the work of Jesus' companions—because Jesus was greater than the temple!

> Going on from that place, he went into their synagogue, and a man with a shriveled hand was there. Looking for a reason to accuse Jesus, they asked him, "Is it lawful to heal on the Sabbath?"

True Rest

He said to them, "If any of you has a sheep and it falls into a pit on the Sabbath, will you not take hold of it and lift it out? How much more valuable is a man than a sheep! Therefore it is lawful to do good on the Sabbath" (verses 9–12).

Five important words

In restoring the people's understanding of the true purpose of the Sabbath—a day for spiritual and physical renewal—Jesus used an important verse from the Hebrew Scriptures.

In Matthew 12:7, Jesus says, "If you had known what these words mean, 'I desire mercy, not sacrifice,' you would not have condemned the innocent." This wasn't the first time Jesus used these words in Matthew. In Matthew 9:10–13, the account of Jesus eating dinner at Matthew's house, He also spoke the words, "I desire mercy, not sacrifice," in response to the Pharisees' criticism of His socializing with tax collectors and "sinners." Let's consider the background to these five important words and the implications for the Sabbath episodes in Matthew 12.

The words "I desire mercy, not sacrifice"—found in Hosea 6:6—echo a major Old Testament theme—empty ritual makes God sick. Rarely did God speak more squarely to any issue than He did to this one.

In Isaiah 1:11–13, 16, 17 we read:

> "The multitude of your sacrifices—what are they to me?" says the LORD. "I have more than enough of burnt offerings, of rams and the fat of fattened animals; I have no pleasure in the blood of bulls and lambs and goats. When you come to appear before me, who has asked this of you, this trampling of my courts? Stop bringing meaningless offerings! Your incense is detestable to me. New Moons, Sabbaths and convocations—I cannot bear your evil assemblies. . . . Take your evil deeds out of my sight! Stop doing wrong, learn to do right! Seek justice, encourage the oppressed. Defend the cause of the fatherless, plead the case of the widow."

"Reform your ways and your actions," God continues a book later, "and I will let you live in this place. Do not trust in deceptive words and say, 'This is the temple of the Lord, the temple of the Lord, the temple of the Lord!' " (Jeremiah 7:3).

Again and again throughout the Old Testament God laments the sacrifice-to-mercy ratio among His people. Disregarding the commands that challenged their comfort zones, the Jews settled into routine and ritual. "Many of them," writes Ellen White, "regarded the sacrificial offerings much as the heathen looked upon their sacrifices,—as gifts by which they themselves might propitiate the Deity."[2]

But as His prophets repeatedly urged, God wanted something more.

"With what shall I come before the Lord and bow down before the exalted God?" wrote Micah. "Shall I come before him with burnt offerings, with calves a year old? . . . He has showed you, O man, what is good. And what does the Lord require of you? To act justly and to love mercy and to walk humbly with your God" (Micah 6:6, 8).

"This," added Zechariah, "is what the Lord Almighty says: 'Administer true justice; show mercy and compassion to one another' " (Zechariah 7:9).

Clearly the God of the Old Testament values mercy more than animal offerings—sacrifice in its most literal sense. But what does "I desire mercy, not sacrifice" have to do with these two scenes in Matthew? After all, animal offerings aren't even mentioned.

Jesus here applies "sacrifice" (Hebrew, *ayah*) to the empty rituals of His day. "Sacrifice," explains the *Seventh-day Adventist Bible Commentary*, "stands for the forms of religion, which have an unfortunate tendency to eclipse practical religion. . . . The forms of religion without the vital spirit of religion, Christ says, are worthless."[3]

Eugene Peterson helpfully paraphrases "I desire mercy, not sacrifice" as "I'm after mercy, not religion" (Matthew 9:13, *The Message*).

What Jesus desires most is mercy (Hebrew, *hesed*)—love for God and love for people. These were, are, and always will be, the two greatest commandments—all the other commands "hang on these two" (Matthew 22:40).

This was the Pharisees' mistake—they stopped at the lesser

commandments and therefore stopped too soon. They tried to keep the Sabbath holy, but they didn't use that holiness to commune better with the Lord of the Sabbath. They tried to keep their minds and stomachs pure, but they didn't use that purity to better minister to the filthy around them. They focused so hard on the "don'ts" that they never got around to the "dos." Figuratively speaking, they didn't clutter their homes and yards so that when company came over, they could serve better. Except that when company did come, they trembled at what might happen to their homes and yards.

Jesus helps people understand that the purpose of holiness, of not sinning, is to facilitate love for God and people.

Unrest over a rest day

Many Christians today say that the Sabbath episodes in the Gospels are evidence that Jesus was not reforming the Sabbath, but rather He was abolishing it. But if it were true that Jesus had abolished the Sabbath, why would the Gospels—penned decades later—still include so much material and instruction about the Sabbath? If the Sabbath were no longer relevant, then why include these accounts at all? (Even Mark, written largely for Gentiles, includes the Sabbath accounts.)

Jesus didn't abolish the Sabbath. He restored the Sabbath, freeing it of the cumbersome burdens man had placed on it. Hundreds of years later, Christians were still resting and worshiping on Sabbath. The fifth-century historian Socrates Scholasticus wrote: "Almost all churches throughout the world celebrate the sacred mysteries on the sabbath of every week, yet the Christians of Alexandria and at Rome, on account of some ancient tradition, have ceased to do this."[4]

The reason that some elements of the Christian church began distancing themselves from the Sabbath was, frankly, to distance themselves from the Jews.

Just as God's salvation rest and Sabbath rest coexisted in the Old Testament, they continued to coexist in the New Testament. While the Sabbath, like anything else, can become *too* central in the believers' experience, this rest day is designed for communion with the Lord of the Sabbath, Jesus Christ.

Today, when both Jews and Christians are asking sincere questions about each other's faiths, the Seventh-day Adventist Church is perfectly positioned as a Judeo-Christian faith community to bring together both groups in the faith that Jesus described so memorably in Matthew 13:52: "Therefore every teacher of the law who has been instructed about the kingdom of heaven is like the owner of a house who brings out of his storeroom new treasures as well as old."

A sin that can't be pardoned?

In dismissing Jesus as a Sabbath-breaker, the Pharisees positioned themselves for something much more serious: dismissing Jesus altogether.

After the Sabbath controversies, Jesus went out and healed a demon-possessed man who was blind and mute. The Pharisees were asked to respond. Panicked, they said, "It is only by Beelzebub, the prince of demons, that this fellow drives out demons" (Matthew 12:24). Beelzebub was another name for Satan.

Jesus responded, not defensively but with a grave warning: "Anyone who speaks a word against the Son of Man will be forgiven, but anyone who speaks against the Holy Spirit will not be forgiven, either in this age or in the age to come" (verse 32). Mark adds a further explanation: "He said this because they were saying, 'He has an evil spirit'" (Mark 3:30).

What was Jesus saying here? In general terms, He was saying: "Be very careful not to say something isn't of God—when it is of God." This is an important principle as we relate to other Christian believers. Even if they may not understand a biblical truth, such as the Sabbath, it doesn't mean they aren't Christ's followers. (Every one of us is growing in our understanding of Scripture.)

Does this mean that we've committed an "unpardonable sin" when we denigrate other Christians? No, of course not. Even Jesus said that a word spoken against Him, as a human, would be forgiven. The truth is, there isn't a mistake in the world that Christ won't forgive if we will receive His forgiveness. Why? Because we can't even *desire* to be forgiven without the Holy Spirit, and if you have the Holy Spirit, then you haven't rejected the Holy Spirit.

True Rest

So what *is* the sin that can't be forgiven? It's simply this: the rejection of the blood of Jesus, the Son of God. As Hebrews 10:26–29 explains it, no "sacrifice for sins is left" when we trample "the Son of God under foot"—when we declare that we don't need a Savior. This makes perfect sense. When we reject the blood of Christ that covers our sins, then the sin obviously remains.

Here's another way to look at it. After the death and resurrection of Christ, many priests in Jerusalem became believers and traveled to an area called Pella, east of the Jordan River. However, as time passed, some of them wavered in their faith, returned to the temple in Jerusalem, and began sacrificing animals once again, rejecting the all-sufficient sacrifice of Christ. Therefore, no sacrifice for sins was left. The letter to the Hebrews may have been directed to these very priests, appealing to them to accept once again "the Lamb of God who takes away the sin of the world" (John 1:29).

---

1. White, *The Desire of Ages*, 283, 284.
2. Ibid., 113.
3. Francis D. Nichol, ed., *Seventh-day Adventist Bible Commentary,* 2nd ed. (Hagerstown, MD: Review and Herald® Publishing Association, 1980), 5:370.
4. Socrates Scholasticus, "The Author's views respecting the celebration of Easter, Baptism, Fasting, Marriage, the Eucharist, and other ecclesiastical rites," chap. 22 in bk. 5 of *The Ecclesiastical History,* trans. A. C. Zenos (New York: The Christian Literature Company, 1891), 132.

CHAPTER 7

Matthew 14, 15

Lord of All

"But even the dogs eat the crumbs that fall from their master's table."
—Matthew 15:27

Have you ever had a teacher who was hard to understand? You might be thinking, "Yes, I had plenty of teachers that were hard to understand. In fact, I never *did* understand them."

OK, fair enough. But can you think of a teacher who might have been hard to understand at the time—but later you understood? In fact, after enough time together, you actually came to appreciate his or her wisdom?

In the old film *The Karate Kid,* a young man, Daniel LaRusso, asked an old man, Mr. Miyagi, to train him in karate so he could defend himself against bullies. Daniel knew that Mr. Miyagi was a karate expert, but when the training actually began, Daniel didn't get the training he was expecting.

Rather than teach Daniel how to defend himself, Mr. Miyagi gave Daniel a series of confusing tasks. First, he told Daniel to wash and wax his cars in a very specific way—moving his hands in small circles as Mr. Miyagi chanted, "Wax on! Wax off!" Then Mr. Miyagi told Daniel to sand his floor, using big circles. Next Mr. Miyagi had Daniel paint his fence "up and down" and his house "side to side." Daniel was ready to quit his "training."

But Mr. Miyagi stopped him in his tracks. "Show me, 'Wax on, Wax off!' " shouted Mr. Miyagi, who suddenly threw punches and kicks toward Daniel. Defending himself effectively against the blows, Daniel realized that the motions he'd been doing over and over (and over) were exactly the karate motions he needed to learn.

Trusting the teacher

In the Bible we also see people struggling to "trust the teacher."

The most difficult example of trust in the Old Testament is found in the story of Abraham. God told Abraham to take his son Isaac up onto Mount Moriah (the future Temple Mount) and sacrifice him there. It made no sense. Unlike other "gods," Yahweh had never asked His people to sacrifice children. It went against everything Abraham believed. He was supposed to take his own child's life?

But God gave this test to Abraham only after showing that He could be fully trusted. "Go sacrifice your son" were not God's first words to Abraham. The test came after God had revealed all His power and faithfulness to Abraham. It was the final test of Abraham's own faith.

In the New Testament, Jesus also tested the faith of His followers. How far were they willing to follow Him? Like the testing of Abraham, Jesus was preparing His followers for a mighty work.

Bread from heaven

The story of the feeding of the five thousand is so important that this miracle and the resurrection are the only two miracles included in all four Gospels. But as beautiful, and often romanticized, as the feeding story is, it also inaugurates one of the most confusing and volatile periods in the ministry of Christ. Why? Because the people around Jesus thought they understood more than they really did. They knew the kind of messiah they wanted. If Jesus had gone with the wishes of the people, He would have been anointed king. Instead, He ended up nearly all alone.

Matthew 14 tells us that Jesus' feeding of the five thousand occurred while Jesus was grieving the tragic beheading of John the Baptist at the hand of Herod Antipas. As Jesus and His disciples withdrew to the quieter northeast side of the Sea of Galilee, they saw the crowds rushing after them. It would have been understandable for Jesus to guard His privacy during this time, but instead "he had compassion on them and healed their sick" (Matthew 14:14).

From Luke 9:10 we learn that Jesus landed near the village of Bethsaida. A small town, Bethsaida, was home to Philip (and previously home to Peter and Andrew). That's why Philip was the one whom Jesus asked, "Where shall we buy bread for these people to eat?" (John 6:5). Jesus was testing him. Philip panicked and said, "We don't have that much bread around here."

John 6:2 says that a "great crowd" of people was following Jesus. Since this was near Passover time, the unusually large crowd in this area was working its way toward Jerusalem for the Passover feast. Many Jews from Galilee, traveling to Jerusalem, didn't want to go directly south through Samaria, so they went out of their way, traveling east around the north side of the Sea of Galilee, south down the other side of the Jordan River, and then west to Jerusalem.

The disciple Andrew found a boy who had some barley loaves and fish. Barley bread was the cheapest of all bread, and barley was the food of the poor—and animals. The fish there were probably small fish no bigger than sardines. These fish were caught in the Sea of Galilee and were perhaps pickled and made into a kind of savory. The boy had his pickled fish to go with the dry barley bread.

The boy's lunch was brought to Jesus. Jesus blessed the lunch and multiplied the food, feeding five thousand men and their families. The people were ecstatic: "Surely this is the Prophet who is to come into the world" (John 6:14). The disciples were high-fiving each other. You can almost hear Peter shout, "That's what I'm talking about!"

Jesus' action of feeding the Jewish people reminded them of the manna God had provided to the Israelites in the wilderness. "The tradition arose within Judaism," writes Jon Paulien, "that the Messiah would come on a Passover and that along with His coming, manna would begin to fall again (Midrash Qoheleth 1:9). So when Jesus fed the five thousand just before Passover, it should not surprise anyone that the crowd might begin to speculate whether He was the Messiah and whether He was about to do an even greater miracle—feed everyone all the time by restoring the manna!"¹

Imagine being a Jewish person in this crowd. You've grown up with stories of Yahweh miraculously feeding the Israelites in the wilderness—not far from where you are. And now this young man named Yeshua is also miraculously feeding thousands of people. This was exactly the kind of messiah the people wanted: a messiah who would satisfy their external needs. At this moment, the crowds were ready to make Jesus king—He was *their* kind of king.

But the King of kings was resistant to their plans for Him. He ordered His disciples into their boat. He wanted them away from the mayhem and pressure. A good teacher will shelter his students from what they're not yet ready to handle. "Calling His disciples," writes Ellen White, "Jesus bids them take the boat and return at once to Capernaum, leaving Him to dismiss the people. . . . They protested against the arrangement; but Jesus now spoke with an authority He had never before assumed toward them. They knew that further opposition on their part would be useless, and in silence they turned toward the sea."²

Lord of all creation

The imagery of Israel's Exodus would not cease with the "falling of manna." Just as the Lord had once exercised His authority over the waters of the Red Sea, Jesus suddenly appeared to His frightened disciples, walking on the water—"tread[ing] on the waves of the sea" (Job 9:8).

A revealing moment occurs when the terrified disciples wondered aloud who was walking on the water toward them. Jesus said to them, "It is I. Don't be afraid" (Matthew 14:27). The phrase "It is I" is another way of translating the Greek phrase, *ego eimi,* which means "I AM." In Hebrew, "I AM" is the name of Yahweh. In effect, Jesus was saying: "Yahweh. Don't be afraid."

Some religious groups, such as Jehovah's Witnesses, argue that the Gospels don't really present Jesus as divine—that He's only a human. But that simply isn't the case. Only Jesus uses the phrase "I AM" in this

Lord of All

way in the Gospels. He's clearly equating Himself with Yahweh.

Stunned by Jesus' walk on the waves, Simon Peter wanted to be part of it.

" Come," [Jesus] said.

> Then Peter got down out of the boat, walked on the water and came toward Jesus. But when he saw the wind, he was afraid and, beginning to sink, cried out, "Lord, save me!"
>
> Immediately Jesus reached out his hand and caught him. "You of little faith," he said, "why did you doubt?" (verses 29–31)

As Peter again sat in the boat, air drying, he could not have realized that an even tougher test of faith was just ahead.

Asking too much

Back in Capernaum, Jesus stood in the synagogue, repeatedly uttering His most shocking statement yet: You must eat my flesh and drink my blood (see John 6:25–71). What on earth was He saying?

Some commentators say that Jesus' listeners were really perplexed by His actual teaching here, that they believed Jesus was literally telling them they must eat His flesh and drink His blood. This view is supported by John 6:52, where the people say, "How can this man give us his flesh to eat?"

Other commentators point out that a Jewish audience operated much more in symbols than we do today, and that they would have understood that Jesus was using a metaphor. According to this view, the hard teaching that people had trouble accepting was actually the idea that Jesus wasn't the kind of messiah they were counting on. He wasn't here to overthrow the Romans or to provide literal manna to Israel. His kingdom was much different than they expected.

Whatever interpretation is correct, the core issue is: How much were Jesus' followers willing to trust Him, even when they didn't fully *understand* Him? As with the example of Abraham, Jesus didn't begin His ministry by saying, "Hi, I'm Jesus of Nazareth. You must eat My flesh and drink My blood." Only after He'd demonstrated His power and His care for His followers did He test their hearts like this. He wanted to see how much they trusted Him as their Leader.

With nearly all of His followers abandoning Him, Jesus turned to the twelve and whispered a heartbreaking question: "You do not want to leave too, do you?" (John 6:67).

"Simon Peter answered him, 'Lord, to whom shall we go? You have the words of eternal life. We believe and know that you are the Holy One of God' " (verses 68, 69).

Against all conventional wisdom, Jesus had traded the opportunity to be the king of millions to, once again, be the rabbi of a small group of disciples. His wisdom is not our wisdom.

It's at this point (following an enjoyable debate with the Pharisees about washing your hands properly) that Jesus made a dramatic decision. He would leave the land of the Jews and enter the region of the outsiders, the rejects—the Gentiles.

Pushing the limits

Once an atheist and a believer were debating the existence of God. The atheist said, "Give me one good reason to believe in God."

The believer simply replied, "Israel."

Truly, the history of Israel is one of the most compelling evidences for God. God chose Israel and led them by the hand into the Land of Promise, entrusting them with His holy laws and covenants.

But Israel wasn't the only people God cared about. The reason God chose Israel was so they could bless *all* peoples on earth.

> This is what God the LORD says—he who created the heavens and stretched them out, who spread out the earth and all that comes out of it, who gives breath to its people, and life to those who walk on it: "I, the LORD, have called you in righteousness; I will take hold of your hand. I will keep you and will make you to be a covenant for the people and a light for the Gentiles, to open eyes that are blind, to free captives from prison and to release from the dungeon those who sit in darkness" (Isaiah 42:5–7).

Lord of All

The two experiences Jesus had in Gentile territory in Matthew 15 opened the eyes of His disciples to the reality that Jesus wasn't just Lord of the Jews; He's Lord of all.

Matthew 15:21–28 records a story of Jesus being approached by a Canaanite woman whose daughter needed healing. This isn't an easy story to understand, because we're without the benefit of vocal tone and facial expressions. At first Jesus seemed to ignore this woman. Ellen White suggests He did this to demonstrate to His disciples the cold and heartless manner of the Jews toward Gentiles.[3] Then, when Jesus did talk to her, His words seemed very harsh: "It is not right to take the children's bread and toss it to their dogs" (verse 26).

What if you tried this approach? Someone asks if they can have some of your chips. You respond, "It is not right to toss my chips to the dogs." You'd get punched in the nose, right?

It may help us to understand better if we realize a few things.

First, the Jews at this time did indeed refer to Gentiles as dogs—bringing the picture to mind of mangy dogs running the streets. But here Jesus uses the more affectionate Greek term for a "small dog" or "puppy dog"—conjuring up an image of domestic dogs kept in the home and fed from the table.

Second, this Canaanite woman called Jesus the "Son of David." This showed her familiarity with Jesus' Jewishness. Like a good teacher, Jesus had a dialogue with her and tested her. Craig Keener writes:

> Perhaps he is requiring her to understand his true mission and identity, lest she treat him as one of the many wandering magicians to whom Gentiles sometimes appealed for exorcisms. Yet he is surely summoning her to recognize Israel's priority in the divine plan, a recognition that for her will include an admission of her dependent status. . . . One may compare Elisha's requirement that Naaman dip in the Jordan despite Naaman's preference for the Aramean rivers Abana and Pharpar (2 Kings 5:10-12), ultimately leading to Naaman's acknowledgement of Israel's God and land (2 Kings 5:17-18).[4]

Finally, it's likely this woman was an upper-class Greek woman who was part of a class "that had routinely taken the bread belonging to the impoverished Jews residing in the vicinity of Tyre. . . . Now Mark's Jesus reverses the power relations, for the 'bread' Jesus offers belongs to Israel first . . . ; this 'Greek' must beg help from an itinerant Jew."[5]

Why should the Jews share their bread with the Gentiles? The woman was ready for the question—responding that even puppy dogs eat the crumbs from the children's table.

We have to trust that Jesus knew what He was doing there. By having a dialogue with this woman, Jesus dignified her—just as He did the woman at the well (John 4). She left with her daughter healed and her faith in the Jewish Son of David ignited.

This wasn't the last time Jesus shared the children's bread.

Still in Gentile territory, Jesus "went up on a mountainside and sat down" (Matthew 15:29). The imagery was remarkably similar to those occasions when Jesus was sitting among His own Jewish people—teaching and healing them. "Great crowds came to him, bringing the lame, the blind, the crippled, the mute and many others, and laid them at his feet; and he healed them" (verse 30). Mark 7:31 tells us that Jesus had re-entered the region of the Decapolis—the same area where the demon-infested pigs had rushed into the water, causing the Gentiles to chase Jesus away.

But something remarkable had happened since then. Evangelized by the two men Jesus had healed, these same Gentiles now had softened hearts, receptive to Jesus. "Jesus called his disciples to him and said, 'I have compassion for these people; they have already been with me three days and have nothing to eat' " (Matthew 15:32).

Many people don't realize that there are two feedings of the multitudes in Matthew's Gospel: the first for the Jews, the second for the Gentiles. In both instances, Jesus had "compassion" for the people.

It's amazing—this image of thousands of Gentiles coming out to be taught, loved, and fed (manna from heaven) by this young Jewish rabbi. Yet this was always God's plan—to draw all peoples of the earth to Him. A startling verse in the Hebrew Scriptures testifies to this: "Are not you Israelites the same to me as the Cushites? Did I not bring Israel

Lord of All

up from Egypt, the Philistines from Capthor and the Arameans from Kir?" (Amos 9:7). Wow! What is God saying here? That He's interested in the affairs of not only Israel but of all people?

Long before Jesus walked the roads of Galilee, He had sent another prophet from Galilee to preach to the Gentiles. But where Jonah had hesitated, Jesus went boldly. He loves *all* His children, and He invites them all to His supper table—Jews and Gentiles, you and me.

---

1. Jon Paulien, *John: Jesus Gives Life to a New Generation,* Abundant Life Bible Amplifier (Nampa, ID: Pacific Press®, 1995), 115.
2. White, *The Desire of Ages,* 378.
3. Ibid., 400.
4. Keener, *The Gospel of Matthew,* 417.
5. Ibid.

CHAPTER 8

Matthew 16, 17

The Christ and the Rock

Peter took him aside and began to rebuke him.
—*Matthew 16:22*

Let's say that you were to ask 250 people who know you to form a circle around you and answer these questions: What are you like? What are your most defining character traits? What, in their eyes, truly defines you?

Do you like this idea—250 people talking about you? What do you think they would say? Would you feel encouraged or discouraged? Delighted or devastated?

Now let's try a different activity. Go online and search for the words "sand magnified 250 times." Then click "images."

What do you think? Pretty cool, huh? Who would have thought that such treasures were hidden in the sand—that when you scooped up a handful of sand, you were scooping up *thousands* of tiny gorgeous shells? All you needed was the ability to see them.

When God looks at each of us, He sees much more than everyone else sees. He sees hidden treasure that just needs to be brought out. We see a beautiful example of this in Jesus' relationship with His lead disciple . . . and friend.

The Book of Matthew

Bold for Christ

The second most developed character in the Gospels is Simon Peter. In more than three years with Jesus, Peter experienced something that no human had ever experienced before—the exhilaration of fulltime life with a thirty-year-old Jewish man who also happened to be the Son of God. Peter ate breakfast with Jesus; walked from town to town with Jesus; bantered with Jesus; exchanged ideas with Jesus; became close friends with Jesus.

One evening they even walked on water together.

Everywhere they went, Peter watched Jesus of Nazareth restore things to the way God had intended them to be in the first place: old men leaping like youth, battered women finding true love in Jesus, wedding blunders salvaged, blind people given sight, captives to sin set free, storms tamed with a word, thousands fed from a single lunch. All this would lead to Peter's highest moment as a disciple—followed by his lowest.

After feeding four thousand Gentiles on the eastern hills of the Sea of Galilee, Jesus sailed back west with His disciples to Magadan—or Magdala—where Mary Magdalene lived. Dared by the Pharisees and Sadducees to "show them a sign from heaven" (Matthew 16:1), Jesus promised only the "sign of Jonah" (verse 4)—which He'd earlier explained as being "three days and three nights in the heart of the earth" (Matthew 12:40). This mysterious prophecy of His resurrection left His listeners befuddled.

Sailing off again, this time to Bethsaida (where he'd fed the five thousand), Jesus warned the disciples against the "yeast of the Pharisees and Sadducees" (Matthew 16:6). The disciples somehow thought Jesus was referring to their failure to bring along bread. Exasperated, Jesus must have felt like getting out of the boat and walking.

No, He explained, He wasn't talking about a shortage of bread. "Don't you remember," He asked, "the five loaves for the five thousand . . . or the seven loaves for the four thousand?" (verses 9, 10). Coming up with bread wasn't His concern. His concern was the influence of those who sought *only* bread—outward signs and wonders—and who missed the *spiritual* nature of His mission.

The Christ and the Rock

The yeast of the Pharisees, writes Ellen White, meant an infiltrating attitude of self-seeking.

> The glorification of themselves was the object of their lives. It was this that led them to pervert and misapply the Scriptures, and blinded them to the purpose of Christ's mission. This subtle evil even the disciples of Christ were in danger of cherishing. Those who classed themselves with the followers of Jesus, but who had not left all in order to become His disciples, were influenced in a great degree by the reasoning of the Pharisees. They were often vacillating between faith and unbelief, and they did not discern the treasures of wisdom hidden in Christ. Even the disciples, though outwardly they had left all for Jesus' sake, had not in heart ceased to seek great things for themselves.[1]

The warning from Jesus must have affected Peter, because by the time the traveling group reached the northern regions of Israel, he was filled with discernment beyond himself. Not long before this, Jesus had said, "Blessed are the pure in heart, for they shall see God" (Matthew 5:8, ESV). For Peter, this was now happening.

> When Jesus came to the region of Caesarea Philippi, he asked his disciples, "Who do people say the Son of Man is?"
> They replied, "Some say John the Baptist; others say Elijah; and still others, Jeremiah or one of the prophets."
> "But what about you?" he asked. "Who do you say I am?"
> Simon Peter answered, "You are the Christ, the Son of the living God" (Matthew 16:13–16).

There was a heaven-and-earth difference in the way Peter identified Jesus, compared to how everyone else had identified Him. All the others named—John the Baptist, Elijah, Jeremiah, the prophets—were merely human. But Peter recognized Jesus was *more* than human, a Name above all names. Where everyone had expected only a human messiah, Jesus was also . . . divine.

To a Jewish fisherman, taught that God was One, this was an earth-shattering revelation: God had a Son.

"Jesus replied, 'Blessed are you, Simon son of Jonah, for this was not revealed to you by man, but by my Father in heaven. And I tell you that you are Peter, and on this rock I will build my church, and the gates of Hades will not overcome it. I will give you the keys of the kingdom of heaven; whatever you bind on earth will be bound in heaven, and whatever you loose on earth will be loosed in heaven' " (verses 17–19)

In his response, Jesus affirmed who Peter was now—and who he would someday be. But what exactly did Jesus mean?

The phrase "on this rock" has been controversial within the Christian church. Catholics interpret the "rock" to mean Peter himself—arguing that Peter was the first pope. Protestants interpret the "rock" to mean Peter's declaration of the "Christ"—or Christ Himself. (Jesus used the word *petros* to refer to Peter and the word *petra* to refer to the rock on which He would build His church, so He was making a distinction between the two.)

Verse 19 gets even more challenging. Jesus says, "I will give you the keys of the kingdom." The word *you* is singular here—so clearly Jesus was talking to Peter specifically. What could it mean that Jesus would give Peter the keys to the kingdom?

First, it meant that Jesus would someday use this humble fisherman to throw open the doors of the kingdom—first of all to the Jews (see Acts 2) to whom Peter would preach the gospel at Pentecost.

Second, it meant that Jesus would use Peter to unlock the gospel in Samaria (see Acts 8:14–25), where Peter and the other disciples had once watched in shock as Jesus chatted with a woman at the well.

Third, it meant that Jesus would use Peter to bring the gospel to the Gentiles (see Acts 10) through Peter's visit to Cornelius and his household in Caesarea.

Being given "the keys of the kingdom" wasn't about Peter. It was about Jesus Christ trusting someone like Peter—and you and me—to accomplish His purposes.

The Christ and the Rock

Crashing hard

Being used by Christ is not the same thing as being depended on by Christ. God depends on no one to accomplish His divine purposes.

Centuries earlier, at a burning bush, the Lord had essentially given Moses the "keys" to lead His people out of Egypt. A few days later, as Moses made his way to Egypt with his wife and son, he was nearly assassinated . . . by the Lord.

"At a lodging place on the way, the LORD met Moses and was about to kill him. But Zipporah took a flint knife, cut off her son's foreskin and touched Moses' feet [a euphemism for private parts] with it. 'Surely you are a bridegroom of blood to me,' she said" (Exodus 4:24, 25).

What just happened here? The simple answer is that Moses was already relying on flesh, not on God. The covenant of circumcision was a *removal* of the flesh, signifying full reliance on God. By not circumcising his son, as God had instructed, Moses was not relying on God.

History was about to repeat itself.

> From that time on Jesus began to explain to his disciples that he must go to Jerusalem and suffer many things at the hands of the elders, chief priests and teachers of the law, and that he must be killed and on the third day be raised to life.
>
> Peter took him aside and began to rebuke him. "Never, Lord!" he said. "This shall never happen to you!"
>
> Jesus turned and said to Peter, "Get behind me, Satan! You are a stumbling block to me; you do not have in mind the things of God, but the things of men" (Matthew 16:21–23).

From being given the keys to the kingdom . . . to being called Satan! Why was Jesus suddenly being so tough on Peter?

Because Peter was being tough on Jesus, Peter was tempting Jesus, trying to steer Jesus from His mission of salvation. By taking Jesus aside and rebuking Him, Peter was no longer following Jesus; he was telling Jesus to follow him.

Jesus said, "Get behind me, Satan!" because, like Satan himself in the wilderness, Peter had become a threat to the mission of Christ.

Mark 8:33 notes that during this exchange, "Jesus turned and looked at His disciples." He had come to save them. He was not going to be tempted otherwise.

As much as Simon Peter had grown in his walk with Jesus, he was still trying to control things. In this sense, Peter wasn't all that different from another disciple, Judas, who also tried to manage Jesus—tried to execute his own plans for what he thought a messiah ought to be.

"Then Jesus said to his disciples, 'If anyone would come after me, he must deny himself and take up his cross and follow me. For whoever wants to save his life will lose it, but whoever loses his life for me will find it. What good will it be for a man if he gains the whole world, yet forfeits his soul?' " (Matthew 16:24–26).

We live in a culture that tells us to follow our dreams—to sacrifice everything for what we want. But Jesus tells us to do the exact opposite; He invites us to give up our plans and entrust them to Him. Peter and the disciples were gradually learning what true faith is. True faith isn't the exciting experience of pursuing what you most want. True faith is the painful experience of *releasing* what you most want. By losing your life, you find it.

Lifted up

The best thing about being humbled is that there's no place to go but up. Jesus was about to lift Peter—and James and John—higher than they could have ever imagined.

"After six days Jesus took with him Peter, James and John the brother of James, and led them up a high mountain by themselves. There he was transfigured before them. His face shone like the sun, and his clothes became as white as the light. Just then there appeared before them Moses and Elijah, talking with Jesus" (Matthew 17:1–3). The Greek word for "transfigured" is *metamorphoo*—similar to "metamorphosis."

Peter's response to the scene was a nervous ramble—"If you wish, I will put up three shelters"—perhaps because it was nearing the Feast of Tabernacles, when Jews commemorated the Exodus by living in tents. Regardless of what he meant, isn't it good to have the lovably eager Peter back?

The Christ and the Rock

While Peter "was still speaking, a bright cloud enveloped them, and a voice from the cloud said, 'This is my Son, whom I love; with him I am well pleased. Listen to him!' " (verse 5).

Peter's declaration of Jesus as the "Son of the living God" was now confirmed by the Living God Himself. The "bright cloud" that God spoke from was highly significant. Just ask Moses—he would have remembered it.

Exodus 13 describes a mysterious "cloud" (Hebrew *anan*) of God's presence. "By day the Lord went ahead of them in a pillar of cloud to guide them on their way" (Exodus 13:21). Later, in Leviticus, this cloud came to rest not only above the newly built tabernacle, but inside it. "The Lord said to Moses: 'Tell your brother Aaron not to come whenever he chooses into the Most Holy Place behind the curtain in front of the atonement cover on the ark, or else he will die, because I appear in the cloud over the atonement cover' " (Leviticus 16:2).

This mysterious pillar of cloud continues to appear throughout Scripture. In Numbers 9:15, this cloud was associated with the time period "evening till morning." In Daniel 7:13 this cloud (*anan*) of heaven accompanies "one like a son of man" as he approaches the Ancient of Days.

Most shockingly of all, in Matthew 26:64, Jesus of Nazareth would stand before the high priest, Caiaphas, and say, "You will see the Son of Man sitting at the right hand of the Mighty One and coming on the clouds of heaven." Caiaphas knew exactly what Jesus was saying: Jesus was equating Himself with Yahweh, who had led Israel through the desert in the "cloud." At this, Caiaphas did something the high priest was never supposed to do (see Leviticus 21:10): he tore his clothes. In doing so, Caiaphas effectively annulled the priesthood, giving way to the new High Priest who stood before him.

Someday Caiaphas will witness Jesus, our High Priest, returning to earth in a chill-inducing way: "Look, he is coming with the clouds, and every eye will see him, even those who pierced him" (Revelation 1:7).[2]

Back to normal

After their mountaintop experience, Jesus, Peter, James, and John returned to the rest of the disciples—who had been unsuccessful in their attempt to heal a boy suffering with seizures and demon possession. How frustrated these other nine disciples must have been. Not only were they left behind at the base of the mountain; they weren't even able to minister effectively to this man and his son. They were discouraged and embarrassed.

While Matthew's Gospel explains that the disciples didn't have enough faith to exorcise the boy's demons, Mark's Gospel adds this statement from Jesus: "This kind can come out only by prayer [some versions, prayer and fasting]" (Mark 9:29). Like Peter, these disciples, too, had gotten overly confident in themselves. Ironically, Jesus healed the boy without praying, but then, Jesus was God.

Arriving back in Capernaum, Jesus and the disciples entered Peter's place for some down time. Peter was stopped outside by the collectors of the temple tax. "Doesn't your teacher pay the temple tax?" they asked.

"Yes, he does," Peter lied.

Though all Jews were required to pay the temple tax, the priests, Levites, and rabbis were exempt. So to take the position that Jesus was subject to the temple tax was, in essence, a vote of "no confidence" in His ministry.

Peter missed an opportunity here, writes Ellen White, to testify to the absolute authority of Christ: "By his answer to the collector, that Jesus would pay the tribute, he had virtually sanctioned the false conception of Him to which the priests and rulers were trying to give currency. . . . If priests and Levites were exempt because of their connection with the temple, how much more He to whom the temple was His Father's house."[3]

We can learn much from Jesus' gracious response to Peter. Rather than humiliate him for his nervous moment, Jesus gently explained his error—that just as the sons of kings are exempt from tax, so was the Son of the Living God. (Remember, Peter?) Perhaps most fascinating is the way Jesus adapted creatively to the course Peter had taken. Rather than simply pay the tax—thereby acknowledging His obligation to it—Jesus got the tax elsewhere: from the mouth of a fish.

The Christ and the Rock

The miracle is unusual—it's the only time Jesus performed a miracle seemingly for His own benefit. But that wasn't the miracle's purpose. By retrieving their tax from the mouth of the fish, Jesus and Peter could satisfy the requirement of the tax—without really paying it themselves! How brilliant is that? The miracle was also a demonstration of Jesus' authority not only over the temple, but over all creation.

Why didn't Jesus fight the tax requirement itself? It wasn't worth his time and effort. He had another hill to die on.

---

1. White, *The Desire of Ages*, 409.
2. More references to the "cloud" of God's presence can be found in these texts: Ezekiel 30:3; Matthew 24:30; Acts 1:9–11; 1 Thessalonians 4:16, 17; Revelation 14:14–16.
3. White, *The Desire of Ages*, 433, 434.

CHAPTER 9

Matthew 18-20

Questions for Christ

"You don't know what you are asking."
—*Matthew 20:22*

Years ago, two brothers in Manhattan began an unrelenting quest to discover the true nature of the number *pi*. As you may vaguely recall from geometry class, *pi* is the ratio of the circumference of a circle to its diameter—*approximately* 3.14. The word "approximately" is key here, because no one knows the actual ratio. After 3.14, the number stretches out to 3.14159265359 . . . and continues on for millions of digits without ever forming any kind of explainable pattern.

The mystery of *pi* taunts humanity because of its ubiquity. "Pi is obvious in the disks of the moon and the sun. The double helix of DNA revolves around *pi*. *Pi* hides in the rainbow, and sits in the pupil of the eye, and when a raindrop falls into water *pi* emerges in the spreading rings. . . . It is one of the great mysteries why nature seems to know mathematics."[1]

The Chudnovsky brothers were absolutely fixated on solving *pi*. In their apartment they had set up a supercomputer that had calculated *pi* to more than a billion digits. In normal-sized type, that many digits would stretch from New York City to the middle of Kansas.

Day after day (to their wives' chagrin) the Chudnovskys sat in their apartment looking for patterns in billions of decimal places after 3.14.

The Book of Matthew

At the height of frustration, one of the brothers screamed out, "We know absolutely *nothing* about *pi*! What . . . does it mean?"

The search for answers

If you could know the truth about anything in the world, what would it be? The solution to *pi*? The secrets of Creation week? Whom you're going to marry someday?

In the final months of His life, Jesus opened Himself up to any questions anyone wanted to ask. We find many of them in Matthew 18 to 20.

Question: "Who is the greatest in the kingdom of heaven?"—The Disciples

Answer: "I tell you the truth, unless you change and become like little children, you will never enter the kingdom of heaven. Therefore, whoever humbles himself like this child is the greatest in the kingdom of heaven" (Matthew 18:1, 3, 4).

To illustrate greatness, Jesus called a child to stand before Him. (Some commentators speculate that it might even have been Peter's child.) Jesus said that "whoever humbles himself like this child is the greatest in the kingdom of heaven."

One indicator of humility is obedience—putting God's Word ahead of our own will. If we're on the *wrong* path, that's because we're on our *own* paths. The solution is simple: we humble ourselves and get back on God's path through obedience to His Word. If Adam and Eve had stayed humble, they would not have sinned. The tree of life and the tree of knowledge were both located in the middle of the garden. Often, life and death aren't far apart. The difference is humility.

Jesus used the subject of greatness and humility to discuss another aspect of greatness—the way we treat people. "Whoever welcomes a little child like this in my name welcomes me. But if anyone causes one of these little ones who believe in me to sin, it would be better for him to have a large millstone hung around his neck and to be drowned in the depths of the sea" (verses 5, 6).

Notice how Jesus compares a young child to a young believer in the faith. Just as He warns against causing a young child to sin, He warns against causing a young believer to sin.

> Woe to the world because of the things that cause people to sin! Such things must come, but woe to the man through whom they come! If your hand or your foot causes you to sin, cut it off and throw it away. It is better for you to enter life maimed or crippled than to have two hands or two feet and be thrown into eternal fire. And if your eye causes you to sin, gouge it out and throw it away. It is better for you to enter life with one eye than to have two eyes and be thrown into the fire of hell (verses 7–9).

Jesus takes very seriously the way we treat people—in particular, fragile children and fragile believers. The times Jesus gets most upset in the Gospels are when the strong are steamrolling the weak. By contrast, Jesus was a shelter for the weak and vulnerable: "A bruised reed he will not break, and a smoldering wick he will not snuff out" (Matthew 12:20).

Some people might interpret Jesus' warning about being "thrown into the fire of hell" as support for a literal place of everlasting torment. But if Jesus is speaking literally about hell, is He also speaking literally about cutting off our hands and feet—and gouging out our eyes? Let's hope not! Clearly Jesus is using the concept of hell (named for a smoldering trash heap outside Jerusalem; it's now a park) in a symbolic way—the smoldering separation from God. Indeed, in the companion passage in Mark 9, Jesus says that "everyone will be salted with fire"—then adds that "salt is good" (Mark 9:49, 50). In effect, Jesus is saying, "Rid yourself of that which causes you to sin. Otherwise, you're going to feel the salt of guilt and separation from God's will for your life."

Question: "How many times shall I forgive my brother when he sins against me? Up to seven times?"—Peter

Answer: "I tell you, not seven times, but seventy-seven times" (Matthew 18:21, 22).

The Book of Matthew

The occasion for Peter's question was what Jesus had said in Matthew 18:15–19 about reconciliation. Jesus had outlined a process of reconciliation to follow when conflict arises between individuals. First, He said, you should go directly to the person who has offended you. If he won't listen, then take one or two others along. If necessary, get the wider church involved. Interestingly, it's in the context of conflict and reconciliation that Jesus says, "For where two or three come together in my name, there am I with them" (verse 20).

Following Jesus' lead, Peter glowingly suggests that we should forgive others up to seven times. Peter knew this was most generous considering that in Jewish culture, forgiving someone three times was enough.

When Jesus responds that we are to forgive "seventy-seven times" (verse 22), He's saying we must *never* stop forgiving. Jesus is serious about the necessity of forgiveness, not only for others' benefit but for our own. In His sermon, Jesus had said, "For if you forgive men when they sin against you, your heavenly Father will also forgive you. But if you do not forgive men their sins, your Father will not forgive your sins" (Matthew 6:14, 15).

Opening the floor

As Matthew 18 gives way to Matthew 19, the setting for Jesus' conversations changes in a dramatic way: He departed Galilee for a final time before His crucifixion. As He headed south to Judea, and ultimately Jerusalem, Jesus opened Himself up in a way He never had before.

Ellen White writes,

> As the close of His ministry drew near, there was a change in Christ's manner of labor. Heretofore He had sought to shun excitement and publicity. He had refused the homage of the people, and had passed quickly from place to place when the popular enthusiasm in His favor seemed kindling beyond control. . . .
>
> But He now set out to return [to Jerusalem], traveling in the

most public manner, by a circuitous route, and preceded by such an announcement of His coming as He had never made before. He was going forward to the scene of His great sacrifice, and to this the attention of the people must be directed.

"As Moses lifted up the serpent in the wilderness, even so must the Son of man be lifted up." John 3:14. As the eyes of all Israel had been directed to the uplifted serpent, . . . so all eyes must be drawn to Christ, the sacrifice that brought salvation to the lost world.[2]

It's against this backdrop that others, too, would get a moment with Jesus up close and personal—Pharisees, little children and their moms, *big* children and their moms.

Question: "Is it lawful for a man to divorce his wife for any and every reason?"—The Pharisees
Answer: " 'Haven't you read,' he replied, 'that at the beginning the Creator "made them male and female," and said, "For this reason a man will leave his father and mother and be united to his wife, and the two will become one flesh"? So they are no longer two, but one. Therefore what God has joined together, let man not separate' " (Matthew 19:3–6).

Follow-Up Question: "Why then . . . did Moses command that a man give his wife a certificate of divorce and send her away?"—The Pharisees
Answer: "Moses permitted you to divorce your wives because your hearts were hard. But it was not this way from the beginning. I tell you that anyone who divorces his wife, except for marital unfaithfulness, and marries another woman commits adultery" (verses 8, 9).

According to Jesus, there was never supposed to be the pain of divorce. It was only because of the hardness of people's hearts that God had, for a time, made an allowance for divorce. But Jesus here restores marriage to its ideal—a covenant never to be broken.

At a time when biblical marriage is being attacked, we find two clear teachings embedded within Jesus' words. First, Jesus says, "At the beginning the Creator 'made them male and female' " (verse 4). Here he endorses the Creation account given in Genesis chapters 1 and 2. There is no room for evolution here. Those who doubt Creation doubt Jesus.

Second, Jesus says, "For this reason a man will leave his father and mother and be united to his wife, and the two will become one flesh.... Therefore what God has joined together, let man not separate" (verses 4–6). Here Jesus clearly defines marriage as a God-ordained institution between a man and woman.

So what does this mean for contemporary culture's gay marriage debate? Does it mean gay people shouldn't have the same civil rights as everyone else? Of course not. Everyone should have the same rights. The difficulty with the gay marriage debate is that the wrong question is being asked. In my view, the government shouldn't recognize *any* marriage—a religious institution. From the government's perspective, all unions (including that between my wife and me) should be called civil unions.

The more relevant issue for the Christian is gay practice, which Scripture calls sin. As with every other biblically defined sin, we are left with a question: Are we going to humbly submit to God's Word or aren't we? Contrary to the message of culture, those who bend and fold God's Word and tell people, "Go ahead—do whatever you feel like doing" are not the most loving people. Rather than hating the sin and loving the sinner, they are loving the sin and hating the sinner. "Woe to the world," said Jesus, "because of the things that cause people to sin! Such things must come, but *woe to the man through whom they come*!" (Matthew 18:7; emphasis added).

The best friend a sinner has (and we are all sinners) is a Christian who refuses to compromise the Word of God. It is far more loving to say, "I love you; don't do this," than to say, "I love you; go ahead and do this."

Question: Should Jesus' valuable time and attention be taken up by little children?—The Disciples

Answer: "Let the little children come to me, and do not hinder them, for the kingdom of heaven belongs to such as these" (Matthew 19:14).

It wasn't with words that Jesus was asked about His love for children. And it wasn't only with words that He responded. Taking the children in His arms, He showed His feelings toward the little ones, scolding even His disciples who thought there were more important things to do.

"The way in which a person relates to children," comments William G. Johnsson, "reveals much about what they are really like. . . . The truly great individuals behave like Abraham Lincoln, whose son Todd felt free to even enter unannounced the room in the White House where the cabinet was meeting."³

How significant that our perfect model, Jesus of Nazareth, always took time for children in a culture that did not.

Question: "Teacher, what good thing must I do to get eternal life?"—A Rich Guy

Answer: "If you want to be perfect, go, sell your possessions and give to the poor, and you will have treasure in heaven. Then come, follow me" (Matthew 19:16, 21).

Jesus didn't give the same counsel to every rich man. But for reasons known to both Jesus and *this* rich man, money was a stumbling block to the fullness of life Jesus desired for him.

Some people might argue that, in this story, Jesus is teaching that we receive eternal life based on our good works. After all, in verse 17, Jesus says, "If you want to enter life, obey the commandments." In one sense, those making that argument are right. To enter eternal life, we do need to obey the law. Perfectly. From birth to death. If we don't, then there's only one other way to eternal life: Jesus, the Way, the Truth, and the Life. As our perfect substitute, the Lamb of God is our surety.

Then why did Jesus encourage the young man to make some changes? Because Jesus wants us to "have life . . . to the full" (John 10:10). Though our good works don't bring us salvation, they lead us into the abundant life.

Jesus notes how hard it is for a rich man to enter the kingdom of God—and yet He says that "with God all things are possible" (Matthew 19:26). He would soon demonstrate this in an encounter with another rich man—Zacchaeus (Luke 19:1–10).

Request: "Grant that one of these two sons of mine may sit at your right and the other at your left in your kingdom."—The Mother of James and John

Response: "You don't know what you are asking" (Matthew 20:21, 22).

To better appreciate this gracious and humble request of the Zebedee family, let's first consider what has happened just before this.

"As the time approached for him to be taken up to heaven, Jesus resolutely set out for Jerusalem. And he sent messengers on ahead, who went into a Samaritan village to get things ready for him; but the people there did not welcome him, because he was heading for Jerusalem. When the disciples James and John saw this, they asked, 'Lord, do you want us to call fire down from heaven to destroy them?' But Jesus turned and rebuked them, and they went to another village" (Luke 9:51–56).

Based on this incident, how ready were James and John to sit on Jesus' left and right? Not very. Together with their mom, the Sons of Thunder were still more concerned about their own glory than they were about the salvation of those around them. How patient Jesus was with this family—and with mine and yours too. Every one of His disciples still had a lot of growing to do. Nevertheless, Jesus assured them that their "names are written in heaven" (Luke 10:20).

Request: "Lord, Son of David, have mercy on us!"—Two Blind Men

Response: "What do you want me to do for you?" (Matthew 20:30, 32).

In Jericho, Jesus would be addressed by two blind men, who called Him the "Son of David."

How would these blind men even know who Jesus was? There's no record in Matthew, Mark, or Luke of Jesus leaving Galilee prior to this.

Questions for Christ

But there is in John—multiple times. John 9 records a story of Jesus healing a blind man in Jerusalem the previous fall during the Feast of Tabernacles. He put mud on his eyes and told him to wash in the Pool of Siloam. During this feast of water and light, Jesus had proclaimed, "I am the light of the world" (John 8:12). Did this incredible story reach the ears of the two blind men seventeen miles down the road in Jericho? Likely it did.

When they heard that Jesus was in town (having lunch at the home of a wee little man), these blind men, too, sensed it was their opportunity to meet Salvation face to face.

" 'Lord,' they answered, 'we want our sight' " (Matthew 21:33).

Jesus smiled. After a long journey full of questions, he was back to doing what He loved most.

---

1. Richard Preston, "The Mountains of Pi," *New Yorker*, March 2, 1992, http://www.newyorker.com/magazine/1992/03/02/the-mountains-of-pi.

2. White, *The Desire of Ages*, 485.

3. Johnsson, *Jesus of Nazareth*, vol. 1, 119.

CHAPTER

Matthew 21, 22

Jerusalem

"The stone the builders rejected has become the capstone."
—Matthew 21:42

For a thousand years, the children of Israel waited at the Mount of Olives for the arrival of a human messiah, the son of David.

It had been a millennium since Solomon, the son of David, freshly anointed with nard perfume, had climbed onto his father's donkey (an animal representing peace) and ridden into Jerusalem as the people shouted, *"Hoshana Lo-Ben Daweed!"* ("Hosanna to the Son of David!") "Blessed is he who comes in the name of the Lord!"

When David's throne was vacated and people lost hope in its restoration, God sent them prophetic encouragement. "In a little while I will once more shake the heavens and the earth, the sea and the dry land. I will shake all nations, and the desired of all nations will come" (Haggai 2:6, 7). "Rejoice greatly, O Daughter of Zion! Shout, Daughter of Jerusalem! See, your king comes to you, righteous and having salvation, gentle and riding on a donkey, on a colt, the foal of a donkey" (Zechariah 9:9).

Then one spring Sunday, prophecy gave way to reality.

"As they approached Jerusalem and came to Bethphage on the Mount of Olives, Jesus sent two disciples, saying to them, 'Go to the village ahead of you, and at once you will find a donkey tied there, with her colt by her. Untie them and bring them to me. If anyone says anything to you, tell him that the Lord needs them' " (Matthew 21:1–3).

The bitterest of sweet

It was one of the most joyful moments in history—and one of the saddest.

As Jesus sat on the donkey looking over Jerusalem, Luke tells us, He began to speak. But then suddenly He gave up, apparently too disappointed to even continue. "As he approached Jerusalem and saw the city, he wept over it and said, 'If you, even you, had only known on this day what would bring you peace—but now it is hidden from your eyes' " (Luke 19:41, 42).

Jesus' sentence starts one direction and then sort of wanders off in another. "What's the point in telling you what will bring you peace?" He seems to be saying. "You can no longer see it anyway."

From His vantage on the Mount of Olives, Jesus isn't speaking to individuals but to an entire community—the chosen people who lived together in Jerusalem: "If you, Jerusalem, had only known what would bring you peace." There's some wordplay here; the word *peace* is hidden within the word *Jerusalem. Salem . . . shalem . . . shalom. Jeru* (*yeru*) can mean "you will see." *Yeru-shalom: you will see peace.* But Jerusalem will not see peace, "because," says Jesus, "you did not recognize the time of God's coming to you" (Luke 19:44).

Why was it that the people of Jerusalem weren't able to recognize true peace? What was their problem? Was it because they were so conservative, so legalistic, that they couldn't accept the grace of God? Or was there something else that kept them from seeing clearly?

It's true that there were strains of legalism in Israel. The five thousand Pharisees had been trying to bring in reforms—without either grace or love.

But in Jerusalem itself, the biggest problem wasn't legalism. It was secularism, materialism, the world. Years earlier, the priesthood and the temple ministry had been hijacked by secular, political, power-hungry people whose only interest in religion was what they could get out of it.

Jerusalem

The secular Sadducees

These secularists, called Sadducees, were more interested in money and power than anything else. The Sadducees rejected the resurrection of the dead, the existence of angels, and most of the Scriptures (basically everything after Deuteronomy). Though the Sadducees administered the sacrifices, they cared less about the temple than they did about the new gymnasium down the street. Years earlier, the author of 2 Maccabees had written: "No longer were the priests interested in the service of the altar. Despising the Temple and neglecting the sacrifices, they would hasten to participate in . . . discus throwing."[1]

Can you picture priests rushing to get done with their temple duties so they could go throw the discus? Goodman writes that the Jews "wanted to adopt and borrow from Greek culture whatever they liked, while despising the Greeks."[2] While Jerusalem might have had the pretense of religiousness, in reality Jerusalem had become a lot like Rome itself.

This is why Jesus, for the second time (the first is recorded in John 2), so ferociously cleansed the temple the Sadducees were desecrating. Rather than simply leave the faith they no longer believed in, the Sadducees tried to drag the faith down with them. Their only remaining interest in religion was power and greed: what they could get out of it. Indeed, when the temple was destroyed in A.D. 70, the Sadducees ceased to exist.

Jesus didn't have much time for the Sadducees, because they weren't serious seekers. When they brought Him their sarcastic questions—"At the resurrection, whose wife will she be?" (Matthew 22:28)—Jesus saw through their fakery, told them they were badly mistaken, and walked away.

The problem wasn't questions; Jesus could handle questions. He welcomed questions. The problem was questions without faith. Without prayer. Without recognition that spiritual things are spiritually discerned. "You are in error," Jesus told the Sadducees, "because you do not know the Scriptures or the power of God" (verse 29).

Jesus' example is helpful in knowing how to deal with modern-day Sadducees—those who:

- are cultural members of the faith, with no real interest in faith;
- clump together near large religious institutions;
- put up with religious practice only if it's expedient for them;
- don't believe that God cares about the everyday lives of people;
- reject much of Scripture;
- deny the resurrection;
- are secular and political, arrogant and conniving.

Rather than enter into fruitless discussions with those who know "neither the Scriptures nor the power of God" (verse 29, ESV), we, like Jesus, ought to simply walk away.

One of Jesus' final parables, the parable of the tenants (see Matthew 21:33–42) was especially for the Sadducees: a story of hardened hearts and the rejection of the prophets (the Scriptures) and ultimately the rejection of the Son of God. "The stone the builders rejected," Jesus said, "has become the capstone; . . . He who falls on this stone will be broken to pieces, but he on whom it falls will be crushed" (Matthew 21:42, 44). Jesus used the sober imagery of stoning—with a final warning: it's better to be broken than to be crushed.

Ellen White writes,

> In quoting the prophecy of the rejected stone [Psalm 118:22, 23], Christ referred to an actual occurrence in the history of Israel. The incident was connected with the building of the first temple. . . . When the temple of Solomon was erected, the immense stones for the walls and the foundation were entirely prepared at the quarry; after they were brought to the place of building, not an instrument was to be used upon them; the workmen had only to place them in position. For use in the foundation, one stone of unusual size and peculiar shape had been brought; but the workmen could find no place for it, and would not accept it. It was an annoyance to them as it lay unused in their way. Long it remained a rejected stone. But when the builders came to the laying of the corner, they searched for a long time to find a stone of sufficient size and

strength, and of the proper shape, to take that particular place, and bear the great weight which would rest upon it. . . . But at last attention was called to the stone so long rejected. . . . The stone was accepted, brought to its assigned position, and found to be an exact fit.[3]

Closely related to Jesus' cleansing of the temple was His cursing of the fig tree. (In fact, the Gospel of Mark sandwiches the temple cleansing within the account of the fig tree.) "Even as a fig tree (a well-known Old Testament symbol for Israel) that did not bear fruit was judged," comments Robert H. Stein, "so also the temple, which represented official Judaism, was judged because it did not bear fruit."[4]

Ellen White points out,

It was not the season for ripe figs, except in certain localities; and on the highlands about Jerusalem it might truly be said, "The time of figs was not yet." But in the orchard to which Jesus came, one tree appeared to be in advance of all the others. It was already covered with leaves. It is the nature of the fig tree that before the leaves open, the growing fruit appears. Therefore this tree in full leaf gave promise of well-developed fruit. But its appearance was deceptive. Upon searching its branches, from the lowest bough to the topmost twig, Jesus found "nothing but leaves." It was a mass of pretentious foliage, nothing more.

Christ uttered against it a withering curse. "No man eat fruit of thee hereafter forever," He said. . . . The cursing of the fig tree was an acted parable. That barren tree flaunting its pretentious foliage in the very face of Christ, was a symbol of the Jewish nation.[5]

The pious Pharisees

By contrast to His dismissal of the Sadducees, Jesus had a lot of time for the Pharisees. He spent hours in dialog with Pharisees. He ate in Pharisee homes. Late at night He plumbed the depths of water and

Spirit with a Pharisee. One day He would entrust a Pharisee, Saul of Tarsus, with the gospel to the Gentiles. Theologically, Jesus had more in common with the Pharisees than with any other group. He knew what a powerful force for the kingdom the Pharisees could be if their humility and love ever matched their zeal. So He constantly pleaded with them to enter fully into the kingdom of heaven.

In Jesus' parable of the wedding banquet (Matthew 22:1–14), both "good" and "bad" people come to the wedding hall. And both "good" and "bad" people are invited to put on the clean wedding garments provided by the host. The wedding garments represented the righteousness of Christ—and everyone needed them, "good" and "bad" people alike. But one of the guests refused to wear the garments, apparently deciding that his own clothes were clean enough.

Realizing the message of the parable, that their own arrogance kept them from receiving the grace of Christ, the Pharisees were offended.

They retaliated with a series of difficult questions designed to trap Jesus; His responses left them amazed.

When they asked Jesus about paying taxes to Caesar, He answered, "Give to Caesar what is Caesar's, and to God what is God's" (verse 21).

When they asked which commandment was the greatest, He replied, " 'Love the Lord your God with all your heart and with all your soul and with all your mind.' This is the first and greatest commandment. And the second is like it: 'Love your neighbor as yourself.' All the Law and the Prophets hang on these two commandments" (verses 37–40). What more could they say? It was the perfect answer. Mark even records one scribe complimenting Jesus: "Well said, teacher!" (Mark 12:32). It was a welcome calm in a gathering storm.

A question from Christ

It was now Jesus' turn to ask a question.

" 'What do you think about the Christ? Whose son is he?'

" 'The son of David,' they replied.

"He said to them, 'How is it then that David, speaking by the Spirit, calls him "lord"? For he says, "The Lord said to my lord, 'Sit at my right hand until I put your enemies under your feet.' " If then David then calls him *lord,* how can he be his son?' " (Matthew 22:42–45, my translation; in these verses, the word "lord" may be capitalized differently in your Bible).

Jesus here was citing Psalm 110, a highly intriguing psalm that was believed by the Jews to be Messianic. Because this was a psalm "of David" and the expected messiah was to be a son of David, Jesus was asking why King David himself would refer to him as "my lord." As Jesus said, if David calls this figure "lord," how could this lord be his son?

In trying to explain this exchange, Christian commentators have sometimes taken things too far. They have incorrectly interpreted Psalm 110:1 as "The Lord [Yahweh] says to my Lord [Adonai], 'Sit at my right hand . . . ,' " explaining that God the Father is speaking to God the Son. While it's true that the first "Lord" mentioned here is indeed Yahweh, the second "Lord/lord" is likely a human figure. The Hebrew term for this second figure is *adon,* which can refer to a human lord or a divine Lord; but when *adon* appears with the possessive "my" in the Hebrew Scriptures, it typically refers to a human lord. (See, for example, 1 Samuel 29:8; Exodus 21:5; Genesis 18:12.) So it's overly ambitious for Christians to declare that verse 1 of Psalm 110 proves the existence of God the Father and God the Son. (Jews reject the concept of the Trinity.)

There is, however, another "Lord" in this psalm. He can be found in verse 5, sitting at someone's right hand. He is the Lord Adonai. (There is no possessive "my" here.) But at whose right hand is Adonai sitting? Based on verse 1, it appears that this figure is sitting at the right hand of Yahweh[6]—because in verse 1 Yahweh tells a figure ("my lord") to sit at His right hand. Yes, but didn't we just say that "my lord" refers to a human lord? How can there be a human lord at the right hand of Yahweh in verse 1, and a divine Lord at the right hand of Yahweh in verse 5? How can one figure be both human and divine . . . at the same time?

The revelation is startling: It's the human nature of "my lord" in verse 1 that sets up the cosmic punch line—the divine nature of this same "Lord" in verse 5. The Messiah is not only from earth; He's from heaven; he's not only the son of man; He's the Son of God. Not only is he the offspring of David; He's the Root of Jesse (see Revelation 22:16; Romans 15:12).

This was the point Jesus was making. And it was about to get him killed.

---

1. Martin Goodman, *Rome and Jerusalem: The Clash of Ancient Civilizations* (New York: Vintage Books, 2008), 105.
2. Ibid., 101.
3. White, *The Desire of Ages*, 597, 598.
4. Robert H. Stein, *Jesus the Messiah: A Survey of the Life of Christ* (Downers Grove, IL: InterVarsity Press, 1996), 182.
5. White, *The Desire of Ages*, 581, 582.
6. Some have suggested that in verse 5, *adoni* sits at the right hand of a human lord, meaning that we've gone from a human at the right hand of Yahweh in verse 1 to a divine Lord Adonai at the right hand of a human in verse 5. (There are indeed instances where the Lord Yahweh, but not the Lord Adonai, is described as being at the right hand of a human: Psalm 16:8; 109:31; 121:5.) While this is possible, it must be asked: Did these figures somehow switch seats? If so, why? Also, if the "Lord" (Yahweh) of verse 1 is the same figure as the "Lord" (*adonai*) of verse 5 (who's described as the "Lord" who will crush kings and judge the nations [verses 5, 6]), would the Lord (Yahweh) also drink from a brook along the way (verse 7)? It would seem more sensible that the human lord (*adoni*) invited to sit at the right hand of Yahweh in verse 1 is also the divine Lord (*adonai*) at the right hand of Yahweh in verse 5.

CHAPTER 11

Matthew 23-25

Christ's Divorce

"Look, your house is left to you desolate."
—*Matthew 23:38*

It was Christ Himself who had led the children of Israel out of Egypt with a mighty hand and an outstretched arm. On eagle's wings He carried them out of slavery and brought them to Himself. "Out of all nations," He lovingly promised them, "you will be my treasured possession. Although the whole earth is mine, you will be for me a kingdom of priests and a holy nation" (Exodus 19:5, 6).

Up on a mountain called Sinai, the Lord proposed. The people "went up and saw the God of Israel. Under his feet was something like a pavement made of sapphire, clear as the sky itself. . . . They saw God, and they ate and drank" (Exodus 24:9–11). When the Lord offered His hand to Israel in marriage, Israel grasped it and said, "Yes, we want to live forever with You in the Land of Promise."

But again and again the unfaithful wife wandered from her husband, breaking His heart. He desired to commune with His beloved, yet her love was like the morning mist.

If Israel's unfaithfulness could be excused by distance—after all, she couldn't even *see* Him—what excuse was left when she could see Him? He took on flesh and loved Israel, but her heart had grown too cold to receive Him.

Matthew 23 is Jesus' final desperate plea for reconciliation with His beloved. Like a shouting match in the living room, Jesus and Israel stood face to face in the temple one final time. "Jerusalem, Jerusalem," He cried, "you who kill the prophets and stone those sent to you, how often I have longed to gather your children together, as a hen gathers her chicks under her wings, but you were not willing" (Matthew 23:37). It was to no avail. Despised and rejected, the Lord slowly departed their shared home. "Look," he said, "your house is left to you desolate" (verse 38). Divorced by Israel, Jesus was now a single man.

But He wasn't giving up. On the way out of the inner court, Jesus had uttered a haunting promise to Israel's leaders: "I am sending you prophets and wise men and teachers. Some of them you will kill and crucify; others you will flog in your synagogues and pursue from town to town. . . . I tell you the truth, all this will come upon this generation" (verses 34, 36).

Who were these new "prophets and wise men and teachers" that Jesus would be sending to the twelve tribes of Israel?

The twelve men He now turned to.

Preparing a new Twelve

"Jesus left the temple and was walking away when his disciples came up to him to call his attention to its buildings. 'Do you see all these things?' he asked. 'I tell you the truth, not one stone here will be left on another; every one will be thrown down' " (Matthew 24:1, 2).

Jesus led the twelve up the Mount of Olives, just as He had once led Israel up Sinai. It was time to explain what was ahead.

" 'Tell us,' they said, 'when will this happen, and what will be the sign of your coming and of the end of the age?' " (verse 3).

"Jesus answered: 'Watch out that no one deceives you. For many will come in my name, claiming, "I am the Messiah," and will deceive many. You will hear of wars and rumors of wars, but see to it that you are not alarmed. Such things must happen, but the end is still to come' " (verses 4–6).

Jesus's answer to the disciples' two questions fills the entire twenty-fourth chapter of Matthew. It's difficult, however, to tell where one

Christ's Divorce

answer ends and the other begins. Ellen White explains,

> Jesus did not answer His disciples by taking up separately the destruction of Jerusalem and the great day of His coming. He mingled the description of these two events. Had He opened to His disciples future events as He beheld them, they would have been unable to endure the sight. In mercy to them He blended the description of the two great crises, leaving the disciples to study out the meaning for themselves. . . . This entire discourse was given, not for the disciples only, but for those who should live in the last scenes of this earth's history.[1]

Most of what Jesus described through verse 21 seems to apply primarily to the disciples and the early church. There were many false Christs over the next forty years prior to the destruction of Jerusalem. There was also a major famine in A.D. 46 and a major earthquake in A.D. 61. Most of the disciples were handed over, persecuted, and put to death—martyred.

It's interesting to consider which of these events the disciples could control—and which they could not. Everything Jesus foretold was out of the disciples' control except for one thing—the preaching of the gospel to the whole world as a testimony to the nations (see verse 14). The same is true for us.

In verse 15, Jesus refers to the "abomination of desolation" (ESV) in the holy place. What does He mean—especially considering that Jesus had just described the temple as being "left to you desolate"? (Matthew 23:38).

Another term for abomination is "sacrilege"—it means to mix the unholy with the holy. The *Seventh-day Adventist Bible Commentary* terms it "something offensives from a religious point of view. . . . The event foretold is obviously the destruction of Jerusalem by the Romans in A.D. 70, at which time the symbols of pagan Rome were set up within the Temple area."[2]

In Luke, Jesus tells the disciples to flee *before* the abomination is set up: "When you see Jerusalem being surrounded by armies, you will know that its desolation is near. Then let those who are in Judea flee to the mountains, let those in the city get out, and let those in the country not enter the city. For this is the time of punishment in fulfillment of all that has been written" (Luke 21:20–22). History records that when Christians in Jerusalem saw this happen, they fled out of the city as Jesus instructed, whereas most of the Jews were left behind and perished. It is estimated that more than 1 million Jews perished during the siege of Jerusalem, with 97,000 more taken captive. "However, during a temporary respite, when the Romans unexpectedly raised their siege of Jerusalem, all the Christians fled, and it is said that not one of them lost his life. Their place of retreat was Pella, a city in the foothills east of the Jordan River, about 17 mi[les] . . . south of the Lake of Galilee."[3]

The language of this warning to flee Jerusalem was much the same as the long-ago warning to get out of Sodom: "Flee for your lives! Don't look back, and don't stop anywhere in the plain! Flee to the mountains or you will be swept away!" (Genesis 19:17). Just as Sodom had become a wicked city, so had Jerusalem.

Jesus describes this period as a time of "great distress" (Matthew 24:21). Does this mean, then, that the Son of man will return at the most distressed time in history? Yes, but verses 36–41 also describe a period of relatively normalcy: "As it was in the days of Noah, so it will be at the coming of the Son of Man. For in the days before the flood, people were eating and drinking, marrying and giving in marriage, up to the day Noah entered the ark; and they knew nothing about what would happen until the flood came and took them all away. That is how it will be at the coming of the Son of Man" (verses 37–39).

Adventist author George Knight writes:

> The great-wickedness interpretation [of the end of time] harks back to Genesis 6:5, which states that in Noah's time, "the Lord saw that the wickedness of man was great in the earth, and that every imagination of the thoughts of his heart was only evil continually" (RSV). Note, however, that Genesis 6:5 is from God's perspective. Matthew 24:37-39 can also be

Christ's Divorce

read from the human point of view. From that vantage point, the text simply says that life near the end of the time will go on as usual in the eyes of most people. After all, eating, drinking, and marrying are normal activities.[4]

It's because we *don't* know when Jesus will return that He tells us we must "therefore, keep watch" (verse 42).

Keeping watch

Within the Christian community, the idea of "keeping watch" is often presented as scouring the latest news headlines and trying to fit them into prophecy. I remember reading an end-time book as a kid that described Soviet tanks rolling into Afghanistan as a sign of the last days. A couple of decades later, it was the Taliban in Afghanistan that was interpreted as a sign of the last days. It's not easy keeping up with Afghanistan—let alone the rest of the world.

But Jesus doesn't ask us to. In the parables of the ten virgins (Matthew 25:1–13), all ten of the virgins fall asleep—and yet when the bridegroom returns, five of them enter into the wedding banquet. Why? Because they have oil for their lamps. "Therefore," Jesus concludes, "keep watch, because you do not know the day or the hour" (Matthew 25:13).

This parable—and the meaning of keeping watch—is explained more fully in the parable of the talents (Matthew 25:14–30). The servants who have been faithful with what they've been given are commended, while the servant who is wicked and lazy is reprimanded. It appears that keeping watch has less to do with following world events and more to do with caring for what God has entrusted to us. This teaching is most clear in Jesus' final parable.

Who are the "least of these brothers of Mine"?

Many people misunderstand the parable of the sheep and the goats (Matthew 25:31–46). We're often taught that at the end of time, when Jesus says, "Whatever you did for the one of the least of these brothers of mine, you did for me," (verse 40), He is talking primarily about how we treat the poor and needy. There's no question that caring for the poor and needy is a major theme of Jesus' teaching, but a careful study of the text reveals that is not His focus here.

To grasp the true meaning of the "least of these brothers of mine" of Matthew 25, let's first consider the chapters that come all around it.

In Matthew 23, Jesus stood in the temple and made a final desperate appeal to His beloved Israel. Israel had rejected Jesus—divorced Him. Looking into her eyes, He said, "Your house is left to you desolate" (verse 38). But Israel's days of rejecting God weren't completely over. "I am sending you," Jesus said starkly, "prophets and wise men and teachers. Some of them you will kill and crucify; others you will flog in your synagogues and pursue from town to town. And so upon you will come all the righteous blood that has been shed on earth. . . . I tell you the truth, all this will come upon this generation" (verses 34–36). Again, who were these "prophets and wise men and teachers" that Jesus would send? They were Jesus' disciples, His "new" Israel.

In Matthew 24, Jesus warns these very followers about what's ahead: "You will be handed over to be persecuted and put to death, and you will be hated by all nations because of me" (Matthew 24:9).

To summarize: In Matthew 23, Jesus turned *from* His chosen people, the twelve tribes of Israel. In Matthew 24, Jesus turned *to* His new chosen people, the twelve disciples and all who follow Him. In Matthew 26, as we'll see next, Jesus would propose to His newly chosen.

So if the focus of Matthew 23, 24, and 26 is on the disciples' gospel ministry, would it not logically follow that Matthew 25 would be focused there as well? That when Jesus says, "Whatever you did or did not do for one of the least of these brothers of Mine, you did or did not do for Me" (see Matthew 25:40, 45), He's talking about the way we treat His gospel messengers?

Here's the clincher: Every other time in the book of Matthew, when Jesus uses the terms *brothers* or *brethren*, He's referring to His disciples or followers. (See, for example, Matthew 10:42; 18:6, 10, 14.)

Biblical scholar Craig Blomberg writes:

> Who are these brothers? The majority view throughout church

history has taken them to be some or all of Christ's disciples since the word "least" (*elachiston*) is the superlative form of the adjective "little [ones]" (*mikroi*), which without exception in Matthew refers to the disciples (10:42; 18:6, 10, 14; cf. also 5:19; 11:11), while "brothers" in this Gospel (and usually in the New Testament more generally) when not referring to literal, biological siblings, always means *spiritual kin* (5:22-24, 47; 7:3-5; 12:48-50; 18:15, 21, 35; 23:8; 28:10). . . . There may be a theological sense in which all humans are brothers and God's children, though not all are redeemed, but nothing of that occurs here or, with this terminology, elsewhere in Matthew.

The minority view throughout church history, which is probably a majority view today, especially in churches with a healthy social ethic, is that these "brothers" are any needy people in the world. Thus the passage becomes a strong call to demonstrate "fruit in keeping with repentance" (3:8). Though one need not see any works-righteousness ethic present, many have read the text precisely that way. Yet while there is ample teaching in many parts of Scripture on the need to help all the poor of the world (most notably in Amos, Micah, Luke, and James), it is highly unlikely that this is Jesus' point here. Rather, his thought will closely parallel that of 10:42. The sheep are people whose works demonstrate that they have responded properly to Christ's messengers and therefore to his message, however humble the situation or actions of those involved. That itinerant Christian missionaries regularly suffered in these ways and were in frequent need of such help is classically illustrated with the example of Paul (see esp. 2 Cor. 11:23-27) and the teaching of the Didache (ca. A.D. 95).[5]

The idea, adds scholar Craig S. Keener, that this passage is about the treatment of the poor and needy is

> not exegetically compelling, although that view would on other grounds be entirely consonant with the Jesus tradition. . . . In

the context of Jesus' teaching, especially in the context of Matthew (as opposed to Luke), this parable probably addresses not serving the poor on the whole but receiving the gospel's messengers. Elsewhere in Matthew, disciples are Jesus' "brothers" (12:50, 28:10); also the "least" (5:19; 11:11, 18:3-6, 10-14); likewise, one unwittingly treats Jesus as one treats his representatives (10:40-42), who should be received with hospitality, food, and drink (10:8-13, 42). . . . Imprisonment could refer to detention until trial before magistrates (10:18, 19), and sickness to physical conditions stirred by the hardship of the mission (cf. Phi. 2:27-30; perhaps Gal. 4:13, 14; 2 Tim. 4:20). Being "poorly clothed" appears in Paul's lists of sufferings (Rom. 8:35).[6]

Keener suggests an additional dimension to this parable:

> In the context of the surrounding parables, "receiving" Christ's messengers probably involves more than *only* initially embracing the message of the kingdom; it means treating one's fellow servants properly (24:45-49). Unless disciples "receive" one another in God's household, they reject Christ whose representatives their fellow disciples are (18:5, 6, 28, 29). Paul likewise reminds the Corinthians that to be reconciled to him is to be reconciled to God himself (2 Cor. 5:11–7:1).[7]

Ellen White also interprets Christ's "brothers" primarily as His disciples:

> Jesus had told His disciples that they were to be hated of all men, to be persecuted and afflicted. . . . Now He assured a special blessing to all who should minister to their brethren. In all who suffer for My name, said Jesus, you are to recognize Me. As you would minister to Me, so you are to minister to them. . . . Even among the heathen are those who cherished the spirit of kindness; before the words of life had fallen upon their

Christ's Divorce

ears, they have befriended the missionaries, even ministering to them at the peril of their own lives. . . . Their works are evidence that the Holy Spirit has touched their hearts, and they are recognized as the children of God.[8]

It's only in a secondary, homiletical sense that Ellen White uses this particular parable as a call to compassion for all people.

The focus of Jesus' final parable—and His final judgment—is *the way we receive those who bring the gospel of Christ:* ministers, missionaries, all who participate in the great commission of Matthew 28. *Our response to Christ-followers is our response to Christ.* This teaching would have made sense to Jesus' listeners. In Jewish literature, the nations—or Gentiles—were to "be judged according to how they treated Israel (4 Ezra 7:37; Klausner 1979b: 200)."[9] Jesus now taught that the nations, including the Jewish nation itself, would hereafter be judged according to how they treated Christ's followers, Jews and Gentiles alike. "Whoever accepts anyone I send," Jesus would later say, "accepts Me" (see John 13:19).

Jesus cared deeply about the church He was establishing. And He had a particular concern for those who take the gospel to the world—ministers, missionaries, all who participate in the gospel commission. *Jesus says our response to our fellow Christ-followers is important.*

Does this mean caring for the poor and needy isn't important? Of course not. Jesus calls us to care for all who are downtrodden. But this isn't how we're saved. There are good people all over the world who care for the poor but who have no time at all for Jesus. In fact, sometimes it's those who most champion social justice who most malign salvation through Christ—and the Christians who preach it.

Our salvation is determined not by our own works but by the way we *receive* the gospel of Jesus Christ—and those who bring it.

---

1. White, *The Desire of Ages,* 628.
2. Nichol, *Seventh-day Adventist Bible Commentary,* 5:499.
3. Ibid.
4. George R. Knight, *Matthew: The Gospel of the Kingdom,* Abundant Life Bible Amplifier (Nampa, ID: Pacific Press®, 1994), 239, 240.
5. Blomberg, *Matthew,* 377, 378.

6. Keener, *The Gospel of Matthew,* 603–606.
7. Ibid.
8. White, *The Desire of Ages,* 637, 638.
9. Keener, *The Gospel of Matthew,* 603.

CHAPTER 12
Matthew 26

Christ's Remarriage

Then he took the cup, gave thanks and offered it to them.
—Matthew 26:27

In the first century, when a young Jewish man wanted to marry a young Jewish woman, he went to her father and purchased the right to ask her. (He wasn't purchasing the woman, only the right to ask.) Next, the hopeful young man approached the woman, offering her a cup filled with grape juice—the cup of his covenant. If the woman drank from the cup, she was accepting his proposal.

At that point the groom would return home and prepare a place for them to live by building an extension on his own father's house. While they were apart, the groom would send messages to his bride via his best man.

Finally, the groom's father (not the groom) would decide when the place was finished. With great fanfare, the groom would rush to his bride, sweep her off her feet, and bring her home to live with him forever.

Is this ringing any bells?

"Then he took the cup, gave thanks and offered it to them, saying, 'Drink from it, all of you. This is my blood of the covenant, which is poured out for many for the forgiveness of sins. I tell you, I will not drink of this fruit of the vine from now on until that day when I drink it anew with you in my Father's kingdom' " (Matthew 26:27–29).

When Jesus took the cup and offered it to His disciples, He was, in effect, asking them to marry Him—to live forever in covenant with Him. He would go away to prepare a place for them—for all who believe. Someday, at the word of His Father, He would return and take them to be with Him forever.

Leaving Jesus

It was shortly after the disciples received the cup of the eternal covenant that Jesus broke the news: within hours, they would all disown Him: "This very night you will all fall away on account of me, for it is written: 'I will strike the shepherd, and the sheep of the flock will be scattered.' But after I have risen, I will go ahead of you into Galilee" (verses 31, 32).

"But Peter declared, 'Even if I have to die with you, I will never disown you.' And all the other disciples said the same" (verse 35).

My students have often asked me: Why did Jesus *tell* the disciples that they would abandon Him? And after He said this, did they even have a choice?

Of course they did. But Jesus knew them inside and out. The heat was about to be turned up, and these still-developing followers were going to drift away—all of them.

Jesus told the disciples ahead of time not to discourage them but to encourage them. He wanted His new bride to know, beforehand, that even if she abandoned Him, He was still going to love her. "In this world you will have trouble," He told them before they walked to Gethsemane. "But take heart! I have overcome the world" (John 16:33).

Let's say that when you were a child, your father said to you, "I want you to know that I love you very much. And I hope you never let me down." How would you feel? Perhaps a little worried about what might happen if you let him down?

Now let's say that your father said to you, "I want you to know that I love you very much. And no matter what choices you make in life, my love for you will never ever change." How would you feel? Assured of

Christ's Remarriage

your dad's love for you, no matter what? That's exactly how Jesus wants us to feel.

Embracing our salvation

Recently I read a survey that made my heart sink. When Adventist young adults (Millennials) were asked, "If Jesus returned today, would you be saved?" 38.7 percent answered Yes; 42 percent, Maybe; 14.7 percent, I don't think so; and 4.6 percent, No.[1]

I snapped shut the magazine, resolving to give the same survey to the thirty-plus students in my "Life and Teachings of Jesus" class at Southern Adventist University. Surely more of them would answer Yes. We had talked many, many times about our assurance of salvation in Christ.

When I tallied the student answers, I felt shell-shocked. Only 32 percent said Yes.

I talked with them awhile—these students I like so much. A few of them offered explanations. Answering Yes seemed arrogant. They didn't feel like they were good enough.

I cracked a smile. "I thought we covered that!" I said. "None of us are good enough, even on our best day. The only question that matters is: Is *He* good enough? Is *He* worthy?"

We discussed the difference between salvation and the abundant life. The abundant life has everything to do with our lifestyle choices, I reminded them. But salvation is all about Christ. If you desire to live forever with Christ, then you will. It's impossible to *desire* Christ without having the *Spirit of Christ*. And if you have the *Spirit of Christ*, then you have *salvation*. You are "marked in Him with a seal, the promised Holy Spirit, who is a deposit *guaranteeing* our inheritance" (Ephesians 1:13, 14; emphasis added).

I drove to lunch, still a little discouraged. Was I doing something wrong? I later gave the survey to my two public speaking classes; the results were somewhat better: 42 percent answered Yes.

I tabulated another question from the survey—"Who influences you spiritually?" The students answered: mother (named by 95 percent of students), friends (75 percent), father (65 percent), teacher (60 percent), grandparent (50 percent), family friend (37 percent), sibling (33 percent), youth pastor (32 percent), church pastor (23 percent), and Sabbath school teacher (10 percent).

When I cross-tabulated these influences with the student answers about assurance of salvation, the most "assuring" influences were (in order): church pastor, grandparent, family friend, teacher, friend, youth pastor, sibling, Sabbath school teacher, father, and mother.

The students' responses were revealing. Parents were major influences—but this didn't often translate to the assurance of salvation. Church pastors were a lesser influence, but a positive one.

Out of curiosity, I asked a fellow professor to survey the students in his Hebrew II class—eighteen theology and religion majors, our future pastors. To our delight, sixteen of them (89 percent) answered, Yes, they had the assurance of salvation. Is this because they think they're perfect? I doubt it. It's because they know He is.

A secret unfolding plan

Christ wants us to have the assurance of His love for us. He's more patient with us than perhaps we even imagine. He understands the battered, sin-plagued world that we must navigate: "In this world you will have trouble. But take heart! I have overcome the world" (John 16:33).

As Jesus and His disciples walked toward Gethsemane on this moonlit Passover eve, He knew much more was happening than they could possibly comprehend.

First, the disciples didn't comprehend the significance of a woman anointing Jesus' feet with perfume. (This occurred prior to Jesus' triumphal entry, though Matthew records it in chapter 26.)

No one in Israel ever poured out that amount of perfume unless they were doing one of two things—anointing a king or priest, or anointing a body for burial. In fact, write Ann Spangler and Lois Tverberg in *Sitting at the Feet of Rabbi Jesus*,

> The word, "Messiah," [anointed one] alludes to the ceremony used to set apart someone chosen by God, like a king or

a priest. Instead of being crowned during a coronation, Hebrew kings were anointed with sacred oil perfumed with extremely expensive spices. Only used for consecrating objects in the temple and for anointing priests and kings, the sacred anointing oil would have been more valuable than diamonds. The marvelous scent that it left behind acted like an invisible "crown," conferring an aura of holiness on its recipients. Everything and everyone with that unique fragrance was recognized as belonging to God in a special way. . . . During royal processions, the fragrance of expensive oils would inform the crowds that a king was passing by.[2]

The spikenard perfume would have lingered on Jesus the entire final week of His life. No one would escape the fragrance of royalty that emanated from Jesus.

Second, the disciples didn't comprehend the significance of Jesus washing their feet. As recorded in John 13, when Jesus unexpectedly got up from the Passover table and began washing His disciples' feet, He was doing much more than demonstrating servant leadership. He was preparing His priests for ministry. "You do not realize now what I am doing," He hinted to a perplexed Peter, "but later you will understand" (John 13:7).

In the old covenant sanctuary system, priests weren't allowed to enter the tabernacle until their feet and hands had first been washed in a basin just outside the tabernacle curtain: "Then the LORD said to Moses, 'Make a bronze basin, with its bronze stand, for washing. Place it between the Tent of Meeting and the altar, and put water in it. Aaron and his sons are to wash their hands and feet with water from it. Whenever they enter the Tent of Meeting, they shall wash with water so that they will not die' " (Exodus 30:17–20). This is what Jesus was doing with His disciples—His new covenant priests. He was symbolically cleansing their feet in a basin. What about their hands? As part of the Passover meal, the disciples would have already cleansed their hands—but not their feet. A towel wrapped around His waist, Christ, Our High Priest, cleansed the disciples' feet, symbolically transferring their dirt onto Himself. He was literally wrapped in our sins.

Years later Peter would write: "He himself bore our sins in his body on the tree, so that we might die to sins and live for righteousness; by his wounds you have been healed" (1 Peter 2:24). "But you are a chosen people, a royal priesthood, a holy nation, a people belonging to God, that you may declare the praises of him who called you out of darkness into his wonderful light" (1 Peter 2:9).

Third, when they reached Gethsemane, the disciples didn't comprehend why this was such a difficult time for Jesus.

It was never physical death that Jesus feared when He prayed that "this cup be taken from me" (Matthew 26:39). It was separation from His Father. Jesus knew that to become sin for us, He would have to experience this. (By definition, anything separated from God is sin.) Though Jesus didn't desire to drink this cup (how could He desire it?), He submitted to His Father's will.

Hebrews 5:7 provides an additional perspective on Gethsemane: "During the days of Jesus' life on earth, he offered up prayers and petitions with loud cries and tears to the one who could save him from death, and he was heard because of his reverent submission." To a Hebrew, the phrase "he was heard" would be pregnant with meaning.

Back in the book of Exodus, these instructions were given to the high priest:

> Make the robe of the ephod entirely of blue cloth, with an opening for the head in its center. There shall be a woven edge like a collar around this opening, so that it will not tear. Make pomegranates of blue, purple and scarlet yarn around the hem of the robe, with gold bells between them. The gold bells and the pomegranates are to alternate around the hem of the robe. Aaron must wear it when he ministers. The sound of the bells *will be heard* when he enters the Holy Place before the LORD and when he comes out, so that he will not die (Exodus 28:31–35; emphasis added).

First, did you notice the single woven garment worn by the high priest? This was the same type of garment worn by Jesus at the cross. The soldiers didn't want to tear the garment, so they gambled for it. Along with wearing the perfume of a king, Jesus was wearing the garment of a high priest.

Second, notice that there were bells on the hem of the robe. "The sound of the bells will be heard when he enters the Holy Place before the Lord and when he comes out, so that he will not die." According to Jewish tradition, these bells were for Yahweh to hear the high priest's arrival. The high priest was heard by God as he approached with the sacrifice. The high priest was always to enter the tabernacle with blood; if he didn't, he would be killed. (This is how seriously God took worship.) The high priest was also heard by those outside the tent. The bells indicated he was still alive. According to Jewish tradition, one end of a rope was tied to the high priest's ankle, with the other end outside the tabernacle. If the bells stopped ringing while the priest was in the Holy Place, it was assumed that his sacrifice had not been accepted and he had died. He could be pulled out by the rope.

So we have this imagery of the priest entering the temple and being "heard." Just before the Hebrews 5:7 description of Jesus being "heard," Hebrews 4:14 reads, "Therefore, since we have a great high priest who has gone through the heavens, Jesus the Son of God, let us hold firmly to the faith we profess."

Though we understand now what Jesus was doing for us as our King and High Priest on the eve of His death, the disciples didn't understand. Their heads were spinning, and a night of chaos lay just ahead . . .

> While [Jesus] was still speaking, Judas, one of the Twelve, arrived. With him was a large crowd armed with swords and clubs, sent from the chief priests and the elders of the people. Now the betrayer had arranged a signal with them: "The one I kiss is the man; arrest him." Going at once to Jesus, Judas said, "Greetings, Rabbi!" and kissed him.
>
> Jesus replied, "Friend, do what you came for."
>
> Then the men stepped forward, seized Jesus and arrested

him. With that, one of Jesus' companions [Peter] reached for his sword, drew it out and struck the servant of the high priest, cutting off his ear.

"Put your sword back in its place," Jesus said to him, "for all who draw the sword will die by the sword" (Matthew 26:47–52).

Two men on the street

Two confused, controlling, grieving men walked the edges of the City of David the morning Jesus was condemned and crucified.

The first man was seized with remorse for his actions—was desperate to undo them. Judas would later rush to the chief priest and elders, screaming, "I have sinned, . . . for I have betrayed innocent blood" (Matthew 27:4). But when his attempt to erase his actions was rebuffed, Judas "threw the money into the temple and left. Then he went away and hanged himself" (verse 5)—controlling things to the end.

The second man was also seized with remorse for his actions. After being scolded by Jesus for drawing his sword, Peter felt deep confusion. Hadn't Jesus just hours earlier told the disciples to sell their cloaks and *buy* a sword (see Luke 22:36)?

As he watched Jesus dragged away and questioned, it wasn't fear that caused Peter to deny being a disciple. It was confusion—and shame. Peter was ashamed of Jesus. The reason he had shouted, "I don't know the man!" (verse 74) was, he realized, that he didn't know the man.

But as Simon Peter walked Jerusalem in the early light, weeping bitterly, something happened. He let go. *He let go.* No more controlling everything. No more trying to steer the Messiah from His mission. No more drawing his sword to save the Savior. From Caiaphas's courtyard, Peter had heard Jesus' words to the high priest: "In the future you will see the Son of Man sitting at the right hand of the Mighty One and coming on the clouds of heaven" (Matthew 26:64). He had seen the high priest tear his clothes as the eternal High Priest stood before him.

Even through his bitter denials, Peter recognized something special was happening. And if, somehow, *somehow,* he should ever be given

Christ's Remarriage

another chance to take a stand for the Christ, the Son of the Living God, he would.

---

1. Leanne M. Sigvartsen, Jan A. Sigvartsen, and Paul B. Petersen, "Adventism Through Millennials' Eyes: How Millennials Relate to Doctrine," *Adventist Review,* April 8, 2015.

2. Ann Spangler and Lois Tverberg, *Sitting at the Feet of Rabbi Jesus* (Grand Rapids, MI: Zondervan, 2009), 16, 17.

CHAPTER 13

Matthew 27, 28

Crucifixion, Resurrection, Commission

"All authority in heaven and on earth has been given to me."
—*Matthew 28:18*

On my first visit to Jerusalem, I'd read how beautiful it was to hike down the Mount of Olives to the Temple Mount in the morning light. But the night before, our eight-year-old daughter, Morgan, woke up with an upset stomach and a strange dream about Mary and Joseph. So rather than hike, we just took a taxi to the Sheep Gate, where I'd noticed a Temple Mount entrance on my map.

As we walked through the gate toward Temple Mount security, someone called out, "Are you Muslim?"

"No," I said, realizing now that this was a Muslim-only entrance.

The guard motioned us to continue on the road we were already on. "Keep walking up the Via Dolorosa—then take the next left."

The road was cobbled and uphill, and Morgan began to tug on my hand. She usually didn't want me to carry her anymore. Like all twinkle-eyed daughters, she was growing out of her dad's arms. But she kept tugging.

"Sweetheart," I asked, "do you want me to carry you?"

She nodded and lifted her arms—my little girl again.

Resting her hand on my neck, she sipped from her water bottle as we trudged along together. In time we turned left, found the entrance meant for us, and spent two special hours on the Temple Mount. By the end, Morgan was rejuvenated and her old self again. She poured her bottled water over Ally's head.

It wasn't until later that afternoon, as I watched the girls giggling away a hot day in a swimming pool, that it dawned on me. The street where I'd carried Morgan was the Via Dolorosa, the way of the cross. Intellectually I'd known this, but I wasn't thinking about it at the time. I was thinking only about my little girl. As she leaned softly against me, my sole desire was simply to hold her, to ease her burden—the strange yet welcome love that helps a parent understand the love of Christ. Somehow, carrying my daughter felt lighter than . . . not carrying her.

Dead set

By the time Jesus emerged from the Garden of Gethsemane, He had the look of a parent determined to save His lost children. He was absolutely dead set on completing His mission, because He was absolutely in love with the people on this planet. There *was* no stopping Him.

While it appeared to everyone else that Jesus had lost control of the situation, in reality He was in total control. The only thing as structured and systematic as the giving of the old covenant was Christ's fulfillment of that same covenant at the cross of Calvary. He would become not only our Eternal King and High Priest but our Lamb and Savior.

After His interrogation by Caiaphas, Jesus was sent to Pilate, the Roman governor, since the Jews didn't have the authority to execute. On this Friday morning, it was Barabbas, the murderer, who was supposed to be crucified on the middle cross. Barabbas wasn't a first name but a last name. *Bar* means "son of," just as Simon bar Jonah meant "son of Jonah." The name Barabbas meant "son of abbas"—meaning "son of the father." Many early manuscripts record Barabbas's first name as *Yeshua* (Jesus). Yeshua was a common name at the time meaning "Yahweh saves." So Barabbas's name was along the lines of "Yahweh saves, son of the father."

Crucifixion, Resurrection, Commission

But there would be a substitute for Yeshua Barabbas. The true Son of the Father would take the criminal's place—cursed and hanging on a tree, a second Adam, naked before God on a Friday morning.

Fulfilling Scripture

Films such as *The Passion of the Christ* have focused heavily on the physical suffering endured by Jesus. And Jesus certainly felt the pain and violence of what was happening to Him. To be flogged was to have your back ripped open. The whips the soldiers used were embedded with small jagged rocks that tore the flesh; many who were flogged didn't survive it. To have a crown of thorns driven into your head and to be jeered at—this would have been a sickening experience. But not for a moment did Jesus hesitate or attempt to spare His own life. Instead, the resolved Messiah led the multitude up the road to the cross—even as they thought they were leading Him.

At the cross, Jesus was twice offered a drink. About 9:00 A.M., just before Jesus was crucified, the soldiers offered Him wine and gall (see Matthew 27:34). Gall was a bitter-tasting poison that deadened the pain. Jesus refused it. Six hours later—at 3:00 in the afternoon—Jesus said He was thirsty and was given wine vinegar raised to Him on the stalk of a hyssop plant (see John 19:28, 29). Jesus received this drink, fulfilling Scripture.

Thousands of years earlier, as the Hebrews were leaving Egypt, the blood of a lamb was taken and smeared on the doorposts of their homes as protection against the angel of death who passed over. The instruction was to "take a bunch of hyssop, dip it into the blood in the basin and put some of the blood on the top and on both sides of the doorframe. . . . When the LORD goes through the land . . . he will see the blood on the top and sides of the doorframe and will pass over that doorway, and he will not permit the destroyer to enter your houses and strike you down" (Exodus 12:22, 23). Jesus was the final Lamb of God that covers the sins of the world.

Crucified at nine o'clock in the morning, Jesus hung on the cross for six hours before dying. Amazingly, for the first three hours, between 9:00 A.M. and noon, Jesus continued His ministry: He made sure His mother was taken care of; He evangelized the thief being crucified next to him; He prayed that God would forgive those crucifying Him.

But at noon something changed. "Darkness came over all the land" (Matthew 27:45), and about 3:00 p.m. Jesus cried out, "My God, my God, why have you forsaken me?" (verse 46). It was during this time that Jesus was experiencing hell. His Father had drawn back from Him, and Jesus had become sin. "God made him who had no sin to be sin for us, so that in him we might become the righteousness of God" (2 Corinthians 5:21).

As He died, Jesus yelled out, "It is finished" (John 19:30)—literally, "paid in full." The curtain in the temple was torn from top to bottom, signifying our direct access into the presence of God through Christ our High Priest. The temple was no longer a holy place; it was now just a place. (Today on the Temple Mount, there's no hint of a temple anymore; it was completely destroyed by the Romans. Even so, most orthodox Jews won't walk on the mount—they're afraid of treading where the Holy of Holies may once have been.)

There was one additional instruction about the Passover Lamb: its bones must not be broken. Since Jesus had already died, the soldiers didn't need to break His legs to make breathing difficult and hasten death. But just to make sure, a soldier thrust a spear into Jesus' side (see John 19:33–37), bringing forth blood and water. "These things happened so that the scripture would be fulfilled: 'Not one of his bones will be broken,' and, as another scripture says, 'They will look on the one they have pierced' " (John 19:36, 37).

Dead, Jesus was placed in a tomb just outside the city walls.

Empty tomb

Our Christian faith centers not only on the cross but on the empty tomb. The majority of people in the world, including non-Christians, believe that a man named Jesus of Nazareth died on a cross. Even outside Scripture, we find historical references such as this one from Tacitus (A.D. 57–117), a Roman historian:

> Nero fastened the guilt of starting the blaze [that burned

Crucifixion, Resurrection, Commission

Rome] and inflicted the most exquisite tortures on a class hated for their abominations, called Christians [Chrestians] by the populace. Christus, from whom the name had its origin, suffered the extreme penalty during the reign of Tiberius at the hands of one of our procurators, Pontius Pilatus.[1]

There's little debate, then or now, about whether a historical figure named Jesus was condemned and crucified.

The hard part, the stumbling block, is the resurrection—the idea that Jesus of Nazareth, who was dead on a Friday afternoon, became alive again on a Sunday morning. But without this belief in a risen Jesus, we have no Christian faith. Paul wrote, "If Christ has not been raised, our preaching is useless and so is your faith. . . . If only for this life we have hope in Christ, we are to be pitied more than all men" (1 Corinthians 15:14, 19).

When we come to the resurrection of Jesus, there are two options. The first option is to view this story as sentimental propaganda written by a few lonely followers of Jesus to keep His memory alive, the way we try to keep memory alive when a well-known figure dies today. The second option is to take it literally—as a news account of something extraordinary.

As you read the resurrection account in Matthew 28—as well as in Mark 16, Luke 24, and John 20—consider the many details given: the initial confusion from Mary; two disciples racing each other to the tomb; another disciple being slow to believe; a gradual understanding of what is happening. Does this seem like carefully executed propaganda or an authentic report of real events?

If you were concocting a fake story of the resurrection of Jesus, there are two things you wouldn't do.

First, you wouldn't use women as witnesses. In first-century society, a woman's testimony was not considered reliable. To use Mary Magdalene and other women as primary witnesses, as all the Gospels do, wouldn't have made any sense from a credibility standpoint if you were trying to put one over on your readers. The only reason anyone would use women as witnesses is . . . if they really were.

The Book of Matthew

Second, if the resurrection story was only propaganda, you wouldn't have differences in your accounts. You'd get your story straight. Critics have pointed out variants in the four Gospel accounts. In Matthew and Mark, only one angel is mentioned at the tomb; in Luke and John, there are two angels. In the Gospel of John, Mary Magdalene is the only woman mentioned arriving at the tomb. In the other Gospels, there's a group of women. What to do with all these differences?

A friend of mine, college professor Chris Blake, once had something interesting happen during one of his classes. The department secretary, Jana, walked in with some photocopies Chris had requested. As she handed the copies to Chris, they accidentally dropped to the floor.

"I'll get them," Chris said.

"No," replied Jana, "I'll get them. I do everything else around here."

The awkward exchange between professor and secretary continued—all in front of the stunned students. Finally, the secretary stormed out of the classroom, and Chris turned toward his class.

"OK," he said, "I want you to write down exactly what happened here—what we said, what Jana was wearing, the exact sequence of events and dialog."

Chris had set up the whole thing ahead of time.

Incredibly, as the students wrote down what had happened just seconds earlier, every account was a little different. I've done this same experiment in my own classes; no two accounts have *ever* been the same.

Rather than cast doubt on the resurrection story, the differences add credibility. In fact, when put together into a single portrait, these supposed differences complement each other. I've never seen anyone reconcile the four resurrection accounts as beautifully as Ellen White does in *The Desire of Ages,* pages 788–794.

Author Jon Paulien notes that there were a total of eleven post-resurrection appearances of Jesus.

> He appeared to Mary Magdalene by herself (Mark 16:9-11; John 20:10-18), and, possibly on another occasion, in the company of other women (Matt. 28:8-10). He appeared to Peter by

Crucifixion, Resurrection, Commission

himself in Jerusalem (Luke 24:34; 1 Cor. 15:5). He appeared to two travelers on the road to Emmaus (Luke 24:13-35; Mark 16:12, 13).

He appeared to ten disciples behind locked doors (Mark 16:14; Luke 24:36-43; John 20:19-25), and then to the same group with the addition of Thomas (John 20:24-29; 1 Cor. 15:5). He appeared to seven disciples while they were fishing in Galilee (John 21:1-23) and to eleven disciples on a mountain (Matt. 28:16-20). Finally, He appeared to those who watched Him ascend into heaven (Luke 24:44-49; Acts 1:3-11). In addition to these narrative accounts, Paul asserts that Jesus also appeared privately to His brother James (1 Cor. 15:7) and to a crowd of five hundred (vs. 6).[2]

Today the empty tomb of Christ is, in all likelihood, housed inside the Church of the Holy Sepulcher. My daughters and I arrived there late one Wednesday evening, just before closing. The dark corridors of the church confused us, and after several left turns in a row, we just stood still, utterly lost. In front of us was some type of shrine with candles at its entrance. A lone traveler walked by.

"Excuse me," I said. "What is that?"

"That," he said slowly, "is the sepulcher of Christ."

What? I was stunned. We were here at the tomb—alone?

I led the girls into the chamber, where more candles cast soft light on a large flat rock on the right side of the tomb. The girls said nothing as we huddled there together.

Somehow I knew this was the place.

Commission

In some ways, the resurrection of Jesus is easier to comprehend than what He did next—He turned over His ministry to His flawed disciples. In Galilee, He gave them the greatest of commissions: "All authority in heaven and on earth has been given to me. Therefore go and make disciples of all nations, baptizing them in the name of the Father and of the Son and of the Holy Spirit, and teaching them to obey everything I have commanded you" (Matthew 28:18–20).

But it wasn't only the twelve disciples to whom Christ entrusted the gospel commission; before ascending to heaven from the Mount of Olives, He appeared to more than five hundred believers. "It is a fatal mistake," writes Ellen White,

> to suppose that the work of saving souls depends alone on the ordained minister. All to whom the heavenly inspiration has come are put in trust with the gospel. All who receive the life of Christ are ordained to work for the salvation of their fellow men. For this work the church was established, and all who take upon themselves its sacred vows are thereby pledged to be co-workers with Christ.[3]

It's true that at times throughout history, followers of Christ have done more harm than good. "What a pity," Annie Dillard once wrote, "that so hard on the heels of Christ came the Christians." The Crusades of the Middle Ages were a dark chapter in Christian history—and in such contrast to the gentle Healer from Nazareth. Yet for every messenger of fear, there have been a thousand of faith—bringing the good news of Jesus Christ to another seeker, another city, another country, another continent.

Years ago I was standing at the Sea of Galilee, where two sets of brothers once fished and a tax collector looked on.

Down the shoreline, I saw two men from Asia stepping out into the water, their pant legs rolled up. Suddenly it hit me: the message of Christ had reached their land too.

Here we were, believers from worlds away, converging at Galilee to deepen our understanding of—our faith in, our love for—the One who called out from this same shore: "Come, follow me" (Matthew 4:19). Rolling up my pants, I stepped out into the water with the other disciples.

Hoshana Lo-Ben Daweed. Hosanna to the Son of David.

---

1. Cornelius Tacitus, *The Complete Works of Tacitus,* ed. William Jackson Brodribb and Moses Hadas, trans. Alfred John Church and William Jackson Brodribb (Ann Arbor, MI:

Crucifixion, Resurrection, Commission

The Modern Library, 1942), 380.
  2. Paulien, *John,* 223.
  3. White, *The Desire of Ages,* 822.

Notes

Notes

FOR FURTHER RESEARCH ON THE BIBLE BOOK OF MATTHEW...

Matthew: Prophecy Fulfilled
by Elizabeth Viera Talbot

The whole Bible is summarized in one word: Jesus! From the time sin first appeared in the Garden of Eden, God had a plan to save us. Throughout the Old Testament, the Scriptures point forward to one important event—the birth and ministry of our Savior. Matthew's Gospel declares that Jesus fulfills each promise made. But he goes even further, to establish from the very beginning how the promises of the Gospel are not just for one small group, but for all who believe!

Saddle-stitched, 64 pages; *also available in Spanish*
ISBN 978-0-8163-2353-1

Journey Through the Bible
by Ken Wade

Journey Through the Bible is a map to the Book of Books. Like any good map it provides an overview that will help you know what to look for as you search for God's guidance through the Word. In this volume, with clear insight, author Ken Wade helps you grasp the central message of each book, from Matthew through Revelation. Other books in this series include *From Genesis to Job* and *From Psalms to Malachi.*

From Matthew to Revelation:
Perfect Bound, 160 Pages
ISBN 978-0-8163-3940-2

Three ways to order:
1. Local | Adventist Book Center®
2. Call | 1-800-765-6955
3. Shop | AdventistBookCenter.com

Pacific Press® Publishing Association
"Where the Word is Life"

AdventistBookCenter.com   AdventistBookCenter   @AdventistBooks   AdventistBooks